A Celebration of Family:

Stories of Parents with Disabilities

Edited by Dave Matheis

Introduction by Jason Jones

The Advocado Press

2021

Published by the Advocado Press in association with the Center for Accessible Living, 501 South 2nd Street, Suite 200, Louisville, KY 40202

www.advocadopress.org

FIRST EDITION

A Celebration of Parenting: Stories of Parents with Disabilities; Compiled and edited by Dave Matheis

Cover design by Melanie Palombi
Cover art by Kayla Hosey

ISBN 978-0-9721189-4-1

Dedicated to the memory of
Chastity Ross (1977-2020)
-
A wonderful person, a tremendous
advocate and a great Mom

Praise for
"A Celebration of Family"

"Many valuable books have been written in the past few decades that describe the lives of people living with disabilities. There are also books about families advocating and caring for their children living with disabilities, as well as stories of people negotiating the ways of a society that rarely takes differences into account, and of positive steps that people with disabilities have pushed for and won that have changed the lives of all people for the better.

"Until I read this book, I had not read the stories of parents who live with disabling conditions who are raising both typical children and children with differences. This is a strong and personal look at the lives I often witnessed with both friends and clients living with physical, sensory and intellectual issues. Now these stories are collected in a book that people will read, enjoy, and, through it, come to see how others have made parenting work in sometimes unusual circumstances. They tell about a possible, joyful and loving experience.

"These stories are the missing link in peer support, community awareness and a broadening openness to lives creatively lived."

Julie Shaw Cole, author of "Getting Life"

"The book is an essential compilation of stories and perspectives about one of life's most important and challenging roles. But like so many aspects of everyday life, people with disabilities are told that the ordinary for everyone else is extraordinary for them, perhaps not possible or advisable. Perhaps they're just not up to it. "A Celebration of Family: Stories of Parents with Disabilities" sets the story straight."

Milton Tyree, Employment Consultant

"This book takes us on a journey inside the diverse lives of parents who have disabilities. Each contributor's willingness to be candid and vulnerable gives the reader a glimpse of the struggles and barriers, as well as the rewards, of choosing to parent (or not). The honesty in the stories is sometimes overwhelming; I laughed, cried, become angry, and celebrated as I read about the roads travelled by each family. Dave Matheis has brought out the message of each story beautifully and combined the stories into a book that is long overdue.

Carol Estes, Disability Advocate

"I think this book should be passed out to teen-agers in the eighth grade for a focus on what love is capable of for anyone at anytime, anyplace, any age."

Donald Stoltz, Artist

CONTENTS

Acknowledgements

The editor would like to thank the Center for Accessible Living, the independent living center in Louisville, Kentucky, for making this book possible. Their support was absolutely essential for this project's success.

The editor would also like to thank the following individuals for their assistance: Julie Shaw Cole for her willingness to review the book, her advice, and her encouragement; Barret Shaw for her help in proofreading; Mary Johnson for her guidance in getting the book published; Gayle Matheis, Carol Estes, Keith Hosey and Jerry Wheatley for their encouragement and input throughout the whole process; Jason Jones for providing the introduction, developing the questions to be used in the interviews with the parents, and recruiting interview subjects; Austin Nugent for her assistance in recruiting several interview subjects; Lee Wheatley for proofreading; Melanie Palombi for designing the cover; and Kayla Hosey for her artwork on the cover.

The editor would also like to thank the following organizations for their assistance: the Human Development Institute (HDI) at the University of Kentucky; the University of Cincinnati Center for Excellence in Developmental Disabilities (UCCEDD) at the Cincinnati Children's Hospital Medical Center; the Association for Successful Parenting (TASP); and the Independent Living Center of the Hudson Valley (ILCHV).

Most of all, thanks to all the people who told their stories so honestly and openly: Alison, Carrissa, Chastity, Christy, Denise, Donna, Gerry, Greg, Jane, Jason, Jerry and Lee, Jimmy, Kara and Adam, Kathy, Katie, Keith, Kevin, Kimberly, Lee, Lindsay, Morgan, Nanci, Norb, Rebecca, Rick and Marissa, Ryan, Sandra, Sharon, and Tom and Junie.

*   *   *   *

Most of the stories in this book are the results of interviews the editor conducted with the parents. Some stories were submitted directly by the parents themselves. A few were combinations of the two.

Introduction

By Jason Jones

"Instead of waiting to execute degenerate offspring for crime, or to let them starve for their imbecility, society can prevent those who are manifestly unfit from continuing their kind...Three generations of imbeciles are enough."

Supreme Court Justice Oliver Wendell Holmes, Jr.

Holmes' comments above were part of the majority opinion in the 1927 Supreme Court Case Buck v. Bell, in which the Court ruled that a state statute permitting compulsory sterilization of the unfit, including the intellectually disabled, "for the protection and health of the state" did not violate the Due Process clause of the Fourteenth Amendment to the United States Constitution. Carrie Buck, considered to be "feeble-minded," was sterilized by Virginia after giving birth to a child that was the result of being sexually assaulted by a foster parent. Buck was the first person sterilized under Virginia's Sterilization law.

Holmes' comments reflected the stance of many in the society of the time and of the eugenics movement. Eugenics is the study of how to arrange reproduction within a human population to increase the occurrence of inheritable characteristics regarded as desirable. Developed largely by Sir Francis Galton as a method of improving humanity, eugenics was increasingly discredited as unscientific and racially biased during the 20th century, especially after the adoption of its doctrines by the Nazis to justify their treatment of Jews, disabled people, and other minority groups (Oxford Definition).

When the eugenics idea was becoming prevalent, people with physical disabilities, brain and spinal cord injuries rarely survived. Therefore, the focus was aimed at those who were intellectually disabled or, borrowing from the vernacular of the day, "feebleminded" or "not whole". Furthermore, it was widely felt that it was not in society's best interest to allow further proliferation of intellectual disabilities. It was the duty of the leaders of the day to stifle diversity that could shake the apple cart and pollute society with the "unwanted". Poor, disabled, black, immigrants, and many other minority groups threatened the utopian idea that gave rise to leaders like Hitler and Stalin.

Today we look at those leaders as horrible relics of the past and cannot believe they could ever come to power; but the truth is their ideas were not isolated in the areas where they ruled. The same ideas were here in the United States, but not usually looked on with the same violence that were in other countries before World War II.

The idea that we could rid the world of the "undesirables" was a very real and proliferate idea woven throughout the fabric of society at the time. This idea gave rise to the institutionalization of people. Insane asylums, poor houses, and other forms of segregated living were simply ways to keep society from having to deal with things they did not like to see. Ironically, people convinced themselves these things were done out of compassion.

Fortunately, for people with disabilities, these ideas began to slowly filter out of society after WWII. However, the laws that were born from the desire to "protect society" took years to find their way off the books of state legislatures. The Virginia Sterilization Act was mostly repealed, but not until 1974, almost 50 years after Buck vs. Bell. The Supreme Court has never expressly overturned Buck v. Bell, but the Virginia State Assembly did issue a formal apology in the late 1990s.

Unfortunately, the perception of people with disabilities being unfit to raise children has never fully exited from society. That extends to people with physical disabilities now, as well. While we now have the Americans with Disabilities Act and other legislation intended to level the playing field in areas like accessibility and employment, parents with disabilities are still fighting to establish the same status as parents without disabilities.

In 2009, Kaney O'Neill, a veteran and mother with quadriplegia, faced an unexpected battle when her former boyfriend filed for custody of their ten-week-old son, alleging that O'Neill was "not a fit and proper person" to care for their son and that her disability "greatly limits her ability to care for the minor, or even wake up if the minor is distressed" (Chicago Tribune, December 20, 2009). Refuting this allegation, O'Neill demonstrated her ability to care for their son. Indeed, she had prepared for motherhood by working with an occupational therapy program for expectant mothers and parents, adapting her house for parenting, securing adapted baby care equipment, and using personal assistants to help her as needed. Illustrating the bias that pervades the family law system, an attorney who was not affiliated with the case remarked, "Certainly, I sympathize with the Mom, but assuming both parties are equal (in other respects), isn't the child obviously better off with the father?" This attorney, who has specialized in divorce and custody cases for more than 40 years, said that O'Neill "would likely not be able to teach her son to write, paint, or play ball." The attorney asked a news reporter, "What's the effect on the child—feeling sorry for the mother and becoming the parent?" (The Legal Program, November 23, 2011)

Other examples are plentiful. In 2012, Sara Gordon, a person with an intellectual disability from Massachusetts, lost her daughter, Dana, 11 days after giving birth because a nurse called DCF after she felt like Gordon did not act like the other new Moms and was overwhelmed by a feeding chart. It was not until January of 2015 that Gordon was able to regain custody of her now three-year-old daughter, removing her from the foster care system. (New York Magazine, January

25, 2016)

In Missouri in 2010, Erika Johnson was still in the hospital when the state took her 2-day-old infant away. There were no reports of abuse, no signs of trauma, and no reason why she could not care for her baby. Erika lost her baby because she and her partner were both blind. Again, a nurse was involved in the determination of a person's ability to parent. Erika had problems breastfeeding in the first few hours. The nurse made a note that the infant was "without proper custody, support or care." It took 57 days, a period crucial to bonding with a newborn, for Johnson to regain custody of her child. (growingyourbaby.com, July 22, 2010)

There are 4.1 million parents with disabilities in the United States, translating to one in ten children having a parent with a disability. In every state, disability of the parent can be included in determining the best interest of the child. In 35 of the states, there are statutes that include disability alone as grounds for termination of parental rights. And, perhaps most disturbing, eight states (Georgia, Kansas, Maryland, Mississippi, North Dakota, New Mexico, Ohio, and Oklahoma) and the District of Columbia allow physical disability as the sole grounds for terminating parental rights, even without evidence of abuse or neglect. (parentalrights.org/disabilities)

Oddly enough, according to the U.S. Department of Health and Human Services, the right of parents with disabilities to adopt is protected under the Americans with Disabilities Act (ADA). Under the ADA, parents are protected from unlawful discrimination by child welfare programs such as adoption agencies. In other words, discrimination against someone with a disability trying to become a foster parent is prohibited, but the same assurances from the federal level do not extend to parents with disabilities outside of welfare programs.

The true sadness of this whole discussion is that parenting is the most rewarding endeavor most of us can ever be part of. To not allow people with disabilities to have the same opportunity is no different than a building without a ramp or not being able to participate in the workforce. It boils down to a person's right to a decent quality of life. And as a parent myself, who also has a disability, I would never argue that my quality of life didn't significantly increase with the arrival of Micah in 2008 and again with the addition of Bryce in 2011. So, the question becomes: Does having a good quality of life only extend to those in our communities that we deem to be "whole" or able? A follow-up question would be: Who are the anointed among us that get to determine what defines someone as whole or able? I certainly do not think I have the right to make that determination.

In the stories that follow, you will have the opportunity to learn about the personal experiences of individuals with disabilities in a variety of parenting situations including biological parenting, foster parenting, adoptive parenting, and single parenting. The challenges and rewards of parenting with a disability will be explored as well as the benefits of parents with disabilities for children, society as a whole and the parents themselves. It is the intent of those involved to tell their stories very candidly for you the reader to see that the joys and pitfalls of parenting absolutely do not discriminate based on any of the things that differentiate us as human beings. Parents are just people trying to maneuver the world while at the same time keeping a child alive.

We hope you can see the similarities to your own lives as parents in the chapters that follow. And if you are not currently a parent, we invite you to use this as a reference when you begin your own journey into parenthood. Most of all, we hope you enjoy exploring the human condition through the words of parents with disabilities.

Chapter 1

Chastity
"I always assumed
I would be a parent"

Chastity (second from right) with her son, Hunter, her daughter, Julien, and her spouse, Millie.

Editor's Note: Chastity died suddenly at the age of 43 on June 23rd, 2020. She was interviewed for this book on May 15th, 2020.

I was born in Richmond, Kentucky, in 1977. At the time of my birth, my extended family had very little experience with physical disability. The community-at-large still had some antiquated preconceptions that my family had trouble shaking – that somehow it was the mother's fault; that maybe it was drug-related; or something was done wrong during the pregnancy. None of this, of course, was even remotely true, but my mother at some level blamed herself for my disabilities. To this day, I think she still feels guilt.

When my grandmother was told of my disabilities at birth, she somehow got it into her mind that I was born without a head. I don't know where she got the idea, but she stuck with it until she finally got to see me. The first thing she said was: "At least she has a head."

Doctors at the time weren't particularly helpful. They told my mother I would not live to two years of age. When I was alive at two, they told her I probably wouldn't live to four. When I was still alive at four, they moved the bar again. This went on until I was 17 when they finally gave up on killing me off.

I owe a good portion of my success in life to Shriner's Hospital in Lexington, Kentucky. Even though I was born in Richmond, I lived the first two years of my life at Shriner's. Every year after the age of two and until I was 13, I spent three or four months there for some sort of surgery. In those days, they kept you in the hospital a long time after surgery.

Shriner's spoiled me rotten. I was born with a hernia and had great difficulty eating. From birth, I was better able to eat in an upright position so someone was holding me nearly all the time. The administrator took a liking to me and spoiled me even further. Typically, she would schedule my surgeries around Christmastime so I would be there during the holidays and get plenty of attention. When I was at Shriner's, my parents could visit on weekends, but otherwise my family was the hospital staff. It was certainly a different way of growing up.

When it came time to go to school, there was some debate about whether I should go to a "special" school or a regular school. It was very obvious by then that I had no intellectual impairments. In a special school, I would not get the stimulation and education I needed, but I would have great trouble physically navigating almost all the regular schools in town. The one exception was the Richmond Model School at Eastern Kentucky University. It was the only 'flat" school around. So that was where I went.

The staff at Shriner's was largely responsible for the self-confidence I developed. They not only looked after my physical needs, but my emotional needs as well. They always told me I could do anything I wanted, be anything I wanted, that my disabilities would not hold me back. As a result, I always assumed I would go to college and have a career. And I did. I have a degree from Eastern Kentucky University in Special Education (non-teaching) with a minor in American Sign Language (ASL) Interpreting. I have worked with individuals with intellectual disabilities my entire career.

And I always assumed I would be a parent. I always wanted to be a parent. I liked kids. I have always gotten a kick out of the high drama of teenagers in particular. I worked as a camp counselor at a number of Christian camps and loved it. I really never doubted I would have kids.

Again, however, doctors were not helpful. They led me to believe I should not risk getting pregnant, should not risk having a child. Then my orthopedist had a talk with me one day. He said: "You've probably been told your whole life you can't get pregnant, haven't you? That's not true. You are perfectly capable of getting pregnant and you are fully capable of carrying the pregnancy to term. You just cannot physically deliver the baby. You would have to have a C-section." That sounded fine to me. Just open me up and take the baby out. It would be a lot less pain to deal with anyway.

So, my husband and I decided to try to have a baby. We assumed it would take a while to get pregnant so we thought we would try being foster parents. I have to say that the fact that both my husband and I had significant disabilities did not cause any problem with the foster care system. Soon we had three siblings in our house: a three-year-old boy, a nine-year-old girl, and their 14-year-old sister. Shortly after they moved in, I got pregnant, just a little bit quicker than we had planned.

I had a storybook pregnancy. We were actually preparing for things to go wrong, but they never did. I remember going into the doctor's office and being around women who were obviously having significant trouble with their pregnancies. They looked at me like they understood I was having a tough time, too. But I wasn't. I was just there for an extra ultrasound.

Our youngest foster child, Hunter, had his fourth birthday coming up on May 3rd. My due date was May 11th, but I am a pretty small person. The doctors did not want me to wait that long. My husband was hopeful they would schedule the Caesarian on his birthday of April 30th. They scheduled it on Hunter's birthday instead. But Julien would not wait that long. I went into labor on April 30th and the Caesarian surgery was performed on May 1st. I had a perfectly healthy, essentially full-term, five-pound, eight-ounce baby girl. My small body would not let her get any bigger than that, but she had no health issues whatsoever.

After Julien's birth, it soon became apparent that we could not handle all of the foster children. The two older ones were placed elsewhere. We kept Hunter and formally adopted him.

It was difficult to breast feed Julien. It was hard with just one arm. But I learned to make some adjustments and it worked out pretty well. She learned early in her infancy to naturally adjust to my physical limitations. In fact, I would have to say she adjusted more to me than I did to her. It took some time, but I learned to change a diaper with one arm and she learned quickly after the first six or seven months to raise her rear end to make it easier for me. She also learned to help me lift her with my one arm, stiffening up her legs so I didn't have to bear all the weight. I remember being at a family gathering once and talking to a small child on the floor. I asked him if he wanted to sit on my lap and he said yes. I went to pick him up with my one arm. I could barely do it. It was like lifting dead weight. I was so used to Julien helping me.

Early in life, I learned that it was definitely a two-handed world. Not only was it a two-handed world, it was also a right-handed world. Everything around us is designed for people who have two good hands with the predominant hand being the right one. It makes it hard for a person who has one hand and that hand is the left one.

I knew my kids would have to learn to do a lot of things without my physical help. I remember one incident at a park. I would take my kids to the park a lot. When I was a kid, I spent a lot of time at parks. I was allowed to take chances, to see what I was capable of, to hurt myself. On this particular day, I was talking to the person next to me on the bench. I did not know her, but I'll be frank, I'll talk to a tree. I think Julien was about two at the time. She was climbing on something and she was getting rather high. The woman asked me if she should position herself under my daughter in case she fell. I said "No, I will never do that." She was a bit taken aback, but it was true. Even if I was under her, and even if she did fall, there wasn't a thing I could physically do for her. I am tiny and I have one arm and one leg. My kids had to learn their limits on their own. They had to find out quickly what their bodies were capable of and what they could do. There wasn't really much I could do for them in that regard. And learn they did.

Before I took the kids out on my own, I had to make sure they would listen to me. If they ran off or ran into the street, there would not be anything I could do to stop them. I had to know they would stop when I said stop and go when I said go. By the time we went out on our own, they were ready. I never had a problem. Like I said before, kids adjust to you.

One time we were at Chick-Fil-A. The kids were playing in the play area and Julien was up at the top. Again, I think she was two or a little older. The person in the cow costume came out into the restaurant and she was frightened. She started screaming at the top of her lungs. There was not a thing I could do. Luckily for her that day, and for the people in the restaurant who had to hear her scream, her brother saved her. He went in and helped her get down.

When I would take the kids out when they were younger, I think we were watched a lot. I think people were curious about how I was going to do things. I never worried about it. I have always been one who would ask for help if I needed it. I was never bashful about that. It takes a village, as has been said, and everyone was part of my village whether they wanted to be or not. I have had no trouble asking complete strangers for help. I haven't always had to ask, either. One time when Julien was older, we were at Wal-Mart buying something large, so large that I really didn't see how she and I would get it in the car. We were struggling in the parking lot and a man was sitting in his car watching us, wondering, I'm sure, how we were going to manage this. As we struggled to get it in the car, he drove over and asked if we needed help.

Hunter and Julien got accustomed very quickly to the attention we drew when we were out in public. We live in Berea, a small town in Southeastern Kentucky, so I have always gotten a lot of attention when I am out in public. I can't move through the world nonchalantly, I always get noticed. Julien did get tired of me explaining to other children how my disability occurred, how something went wrong when I was inside my Mommy. I think she was about four when she cut me off once and decided to explain it herself. Her story got turned around a bit. It came out as something went wrong with me when she was inside my tummy. Since my arm and leg did not actually fall off when I got pregnant, I had to explain that was not quite accurate. When talking to young kids I have learned that the real explanation would not always make sense to them so I started telling kids who were just meeting me that I was a transformer. They tend to like that explanation a lot better.

I think it is more difficult to be a mother with a disability than a father with a disability. I think it reflects society's continuing bias that women are the primary caregivers and bear more responsibility for the health and welfare of their children. There are just different expectations and assumptions for mothers than there are for fathers. I think there is a feeling among many people that if you can't do it all for your kids, why would you have any children at all? But my kids and I learned to adjust to each other. I have had support from two different spouses and, like I said, everyone is part of my village. We have done just fine.

I am certainly grateful to have had children and especially grateful that I was able to safely become pregnant and have a healthy baby. There are some people who cannot do that without great risk. I don't believe anyone should try to have a child if it will endanger their health or life in any way. Women with physical disabilities need to know their limitations. They need to have the best information before making such a decision.

I will be honest. In the end, if you suck as a person, you are going to suck as a parent, whether you have a disability or not. If you are compassionate and caring and nurturing as a person, you will be like that as a parent, too.

Chapter 2

Adam and Kara
Our Road to Parenthood as
Two Parents with Disabilities

By Kara B. Ayers, PhD

Kara and Adam with their three children, Hannah, Riley and Eli

Parenting is a dream that many people with disabilities aren't allowed to dream. There are countless messages around us - both bold, explicit ones and more subversive ones - that tell us we are not ideal people to raise children and that we should look other places for a fulfilling life. My husband, Adam, and I - both people with disabilities - definitely heard those messages and still do. We are fortunate in so many ways that we have been able to chart our own course and define what family means to us.

I was born in Kentucky and my husband in the Cincinnati area. We were born just about a year apart. We both have Osteogenesis Imperfecta (OI). OI causes short stature. We are both little people. The most prominent characteristic of OI, however, is bones that break easier than most. During my childhood, I broke around 75 bones. OI also typically necessitates multiple surgeries to repair fractures, but also to implant metal rods inside the long bones to help them grow straight and prevent break-through fractures. Adam and I have each had more than a dozen surgeries. There is a great deal of pain associated with OI, but also lessons of resilience and grit.

OI is a genetic disability. For most people, who don't have a partner with OI, there is a 50/50 chance of passing on OI to biological children. For Adam and me, that chance increases to 75% and becomes a little more complicated. To break it down, there's a 25% chance that our biological child will inherit Adam's type of OI, a 25% chance my type of OI, a 25% chance a child would inherit both types, and a 25% chance of inheriting no OI. Everyone has different feelings about these odds. Adam and I were most concerned about the 25% chance of double dominance, inheriting 2 forms of OI, because there is little known about these outcomes, but it's thought that a baby with double dominance would be unlikely to survive.

Any and all decisions around parenting are complicated, but from a quick description of just genetics, it's easy to see how parenting decisions with disability become incredibly complex long before a baby's arrival. The nature of my disability has meant that planning is a way of life. I have a deep need to know what to expect even when there's usually not a model for me to follow and often no way to really know. To prepare for the prospect of parenthood, I looked to other parents with OI and parents with other disabilities to learn from their perspectives. A person's disability identity factors considerably into how they navigate parenting decisions. Our family views disability as a key part of who we are - both one to celebrate and one that brings unique challenges. We see disability as a culture and as an inherent part of human diversity, which we believe strengthens society.

Welcoming Hannah, Our First Child

We had our first child, Hannah, in 2010. We pursued genetic testing because we were eager to learn whether or not she had OI so we could be best prepared for her arrival and future. Genetic testing, though, only provided partial answers. We knew she didn't have Adam's type, which also eliminated the chance of double dominance. We watched ultrasounds carefully. Our doctors felt fairly confident that she didn't show signs of OI, but we decided to proceed with a birth plan under the assumption she did to aim for her safety no matter what. Hannah was born on one of the sunniest mornings I've ever seen. She was a confident and calm little being from the start and was way too easy on us with her nearly constant smiles and even temperament.

Adam and I figured out our way through the infant stages. I found ways to transfer Hannah to and from different levels and we adapted to her growing size and weight as we all learned and relearned skills together. We used strollers at times others might carry a car seat inside a building or house, but mostly she rode comfortably in our laps. With a twist of irony, we seem to raise early walkers. Hannah and her later-to-come sister would walk before they were 10 months old. The challenges of toddlerhood, especially navigating in the community, are a bit steeper. We carefully considered where we went for safety and worked hard to ensure she'd stay with us when in crowds.

Adopting as Parents with Disabilities

Adam and I both relish our relationships with our siblings. As Hannah grew, we wondered how we might provide that connection in her life. We'd both thought about adoption prior to even meeting each other and began learning more about how many children with disabilities around the world are without families. We were drawn to the picture of a little boy in China with a pseudonym of Danny. He was six years old and had achondroplasia, the most common form of dwarfism. We felt confident with our orthopedic knowledge that we could navigate the medical treatment this little boy would need for his physical development. By this time, I'd just finished my doctorate in psychology. I felt equipped to take on the challenge of building attachment and helping to facilitate healing from trauma. Adam and I had friends with achondroplasia and we looked forward to welcoming this boy into our family as a son, but also into a community as a cherished member.

In the summer of 2014, we flew to China to adopt our son, Eli. Our agency had helped several other couples with dwarfism adopt but we were the first - to their knowledge - to both use wheelchairs full time for our mobility. Navigating China was a harrowing experience. My in-laws were gracious enough to accompany us. They provided help with some inaccessible spots and helped us keep a very rambunctious now seven-year-old boy busy. Our time in China was exhilarating as I tried to soak in everything I could about Eli's roots. At the same time, I was terrified that something/someone in the process would doubt our abilities as parents and end our opportunity to become a family. When the plane landed home in Cincinnati and Eli and Hannah embraced, I finally felt like I could fully breathe.

The following months and years were filled with countless "firsts" for Eli that many people take for granted. His bravery to try new things in a world and with people completely new to him was unmatched. He started school only a couple weeks after coming home. He made new friends and met his extended family. His sister was his most adored teacher and they played from morning until night. We began the long process to get Eli's previously unaddressed medical needs met. We've shared our own experiences and coping strategies as he's faced multiple surgeries since coming home.

Party of Five: Welcoming Riley

Two years after Eli joined our family, we learned there was one more Ayers awaiting her arrival. My pregnancy with Riley was more difficult physically. At 36 and still just over 4 feet tall, I felt more uncomfortable and had difficulty sleeping earlier in the process. There was also the challenge of balancing the needs of two other active, energetic kids who weren't fond of the idea of slowing down while I tended to their growing little sister. Even with all this, I felt incredibly privileged to be able to grow another human again! She was much more active than Hannah had been, kicking and rolling almost constantly. We didn't pursue genetic testing with Riley, deciding instead to watch ultrasounds and repeat the birth planning process with the assumption that she did have OI. It feels strange to say "against the odds" Riley didn't have OI because I worry that it feeds into the cliché stereotypes that something was overcome or beaten. At the same time, the odds were such that she would have OI and she doesn't. It is miraculous because she is exactly who she was intended to be.

Ableism and Disability Pride as a Family

Our trio is now 13, 10, and almost 4. Through baseball games, gymnastics meets, and school concerts, we blazed our own trail in our community. There have definitely been bumps along the way. It is a frequent conversation in our home about why people stare or ask intrusive questions when we're simply out and about living our lives. We talk about ableism because it is a reality of our lives. Our children have witnessed the way people sometimes speak to us with an annoyed tone when we're simply seeking basic access. We've experienced parents of friends who eagerly invite our children to their home but aren't comfortable with their children coming to ours. We do our best to teach a balance of avid advocacy, a commitment to education when we're up for it, and self-care when we aren't. Neither my children, nor I, were born to educate others. Sometimes though, it can be rewarding both in the short-term and long-term. We're also grateful for the opportunities to celebrate who we are. We have friends, experiences, and perspectives that we never would have had otherwise. Disability culture is also alive and well in our home. We are proud of who we are. We know the courage that standing out can demand and we also know the rewards for doing so are that much sweeter.

Chapter 3

Jason
"The toughest job on the planet"

*Jason lives in Lexington, Kentucky, with his wife Jessica
and their sons Micah and Bryce*

When I was about a year old, my family moved from Youngstown, Ohio, where I was born, to Louisville, Kentucky, so my father could attend the Southern Baptist Seminary. After he was finished at the Seminary, he took a church in southern Tennessee. There were five of us, my father, my mother, my sister and brother, and me. My dad was a Southern Baptist preacher, which if you knew him now would shock you because he is very, very liberal. It was still possible then to be a liberal and a Baptist minister at the same time. He was the guy that would marry somebody who had been divorced, who thought women deserved a bigger role in the church, and who started a black church in a racially divided community. My dad hated discrimination of any kind. I grew up with the belief that we're all equal in the eyes of God. It was a cool way to grow up. I had no idea then, as a very privileged white kid, that at some point, I would need to be involved in a fight for my own equality.

My injury occurred on April 21, 1990. By that time, we had moved to Somerset in Southern Kentucky. As a sophomore in high school, I played four sports – baseball, basketball, football, and golf. I started on the varsity basketball team. I was already getting scholarship offers in football. That spring, I was high jumping at a track meet. I landed on my head. My body flipped over and I knew right away it was very serious. I was in the hospital for about 40 days and then went to rehab for about three or four months. This was just prior to my sixteenth birthday. I turned 16 on June 14. I was a quadriplegic.

From there I went on to finish high school, then to college and just had sort of a normal life. I had great parents that really didn't treat me any differently and just went out there and fought for me. I learned a lot early on about disability and what it meant. The ADA was passed right after I got hurt and I thank God for that. When I first tried to go back to high school, the school system didn't want me to go. They wanted me to wait until a new school being built across town was finished. That was expected to take another year and a half. It would be more accessible. But who wants to sit out of school for over a year? My dad fought every day, more than he should have had to, but he fought hard and locked horns with the powers that be to get me back in high school. I ended up missing only the end of my sophomore year and just the first few weeks of my junior year. The school had somebody go with me to class. They let me have a student in each class to do the writing and other things for me since I have only very limited movement from the chest down, nothing really functional.

From high school, I went on to Georgetown (Kentucky) College and for two and a half semesters I had no setbacks. Then I had a blood clot in the spinal column, something relatively common with spinal cord injuries. I had to have surgery. That set me back a little bit. When I came back from that, I took some classes in Somerset at the community college and then decided I was going to be serious and finish my degree.

I went to Eastern Kentucky University and obtained a degree in mass communications. I worked as an editor for a small-town newspaper for a couple of years. Then this state vocational rehabilitation administrator met me at a job fair in Somerset. She told me "You need to work for us."

You don't realize how much the decisions you make will affect where you will end up. I was still young, about 27 years old. I went into the interview, never fully engaged in the idea that I could be moving from Somerset to Lexington. Somerset was a small town. I knew my surroundings, my doctors were there, my support systems were there, and my parents were there. Even such things as labor were cheaper. I could hire an attendant in Somerset for a lot less than I could in Lexington. I took the chance and ended up in the central office of the Kentucky Office of Vocational Rehabilitation. I give that state administrator a lot of credit for just kind of pulling me out of there and giving me the kind of support to be able to do that. That summer, I moved to a house in Lexington.

About three or four years later, I met my future wife, Jessica, at church. I knew pretty quickly that there was something different about her. I tried my best to sabotage the relationship every step of the way, but she wasn't having it. We got married and had our first son, Micah, in 2008. Three years later we had Bryce. I can't imagine life without them at this point. Kids are the toughest things in the world and the best things in the world at the same time. I think most parents would agree with that. They are a 24/7 job. Parenting with or without a disability is the toughest job on the planet. When you think about it, parenting is one of the only things you will ever do without knowing what the results are going be for 20 years.

After I got hurt, I had five things that I was determined to do. I wasn't sure if any of them were attainable. The big one was to finish high school. Then I wanted to go to college, and then I wanted to find a good job, somewhere where I felt like I was contributing in some way. I wanted to get married. And the fifth thing was I wanted to have kids. After Micah and Bryce were born, it was all great, I am kind of playing on the house's money now.

Acquiring a significant disability did not alter my desire to have children. I did realize there were a lot of things I wouldn't be able to do. I knew my Dad's role in my own life and sort of knew his Dad's role in his life. I knew mine would be different in the lives of my children. It would look different and it would be different for my kids. Could I be an effective parent? Yes. Could I do everything I would like to do? No. I had to find a balance in my own mind before we went down that road.

The earliest conversation we had about having kids was when we were dating. Jessica was born to be a mom and that's all she ever wanted to do. She was trained in early childhood education and she absolutely loved it. It was what she did so our ability to have children was a concern for her. She told me later that one of our close friends asked,

"Can he have kids?" We were getting very serious. We had been dating for four or five months. She had done some research. I think that may have been the tipping point where I knew that she and I were going to be okay and our real future was beginning because she wasn't afraid to ask the questions. I always wanted to have kids, but with Jess, I really didn't have a choice.

Honestly, we got pregnant easily. I didn't realize it was going to be that easy. We always just assumed there was going to be more to it, you know, like fertility clinics and that kind of thing, but there just wasn't. It was, hey, guess what, you're pregnant now. It's one thing that quadriplegics have over a lot of spinal cord injuries. We tend to be able to do things like that a little bit better.

The toughest thing for me, I think, is probably the affection. I'm a big hugger, I like to be hugged and I like to dish it out. I really like touch and not being able to touch is difficult. I struggle with things like that when the kids get hurt, not being able to scoop them up and hold them. Once, when my youngest kid was a year old, he fell face first out of a shopping cart, did a flip and landed on his back. This was one of many such incidents with this kid. If you blinked, he was going to fall off something, just crazy stuff. I couldn't do anything for him. I still struggle with that, the physical side of things. I wouldn't be able to teach my kids to throw a baseball or to play every sport that I loved so we found things that are easier to do like basketball. It's a better sport to watch because it's indoors. I can be easily affected by the temperature outside. My youngest, that's what he does. And my oldest plays golf where you can go at your own pace. We find places where they're accessible so we can play.

The other thing that has bothered me is that Jess has had to do all the physical work of parenting. Most nights, I was waking up, but she was getting up. When they were little, it was just hard. Children can be hard on a marriage anyway. Our first child was super colicky. He cried all the time. And man, I just wanted to crawl out of the house, but she was up with him a lot. She could hold him and soothe him and all that stuff. I never changed a diaper, but I'm getting it now because I tend to be the main source of attention of the boys when we go out.

My parents were great parents and that laid the groundwork for me being a parent. Also, for me, I had a lot of help from a friend, Lee (see Chapter 5), who also has a spinal cord injury. I don't think I can really give him enough credit. We're close to the same age. When he and his wife got pregnant, I was around him a lot. I got to see the process they went through and how they dealt with things. Every time I saw him, I got an update on the way things were going. When Jess and I got to where we were going down that road, I relied on Lee a lot. He wasn't a guy I called in the middle of night to ask what the hell do I do, this kid won't stop crying. That's not what he was at all. He was a very informal mentor as another quadriplegic. Lee mostly didn't offer advice as much as he just told me what was going on. I would just listen. I remember when his daughter was able to put on her own seatbelt in the car and that was such a huge deal because then Lee could take her places on his own. I don't drive, but Lee does. It was such a huge deal for him. It was just hearing him say that she turned five years old and could get herself in the car, his life changed for the better.

If a person with a disability wants to be a parent, they should seek out somebody who has done it and talk to them. If you get into parenting and think you're going to do it well, and you assume that someone else you see whose kids are pretty good and they are doing it well, first of all, you're nuts. Who knows what good parenting is? None of us do. None of us can get it all right. Like I said, you won't know for 20 years if the cake is done. It may still be soggy in the middle. I think it's so important to get involved with other people with kids. Just develop those friendships. Don't be afraid to ask. Find somebody who will be brutally honest with you. Find somebody not afraid to tell you, dude, watch all the movies you can now and get all the sleep you can because that shit is over for the next couple of years.

Honestly, I'm not too good to say this, but before I had kids, I thought, yeah, I got this. You soon learn that they tend to dictate things to you more than you can control them. It's a good day when you figure that out and you just have to let things sort of happen. You are more of a shepherd than you are a person that's just going to make things happen exactly like you want. And what are things supposed to look like in the first place? It always comes down to support structure. Surround yourself with people that can help, people that can give you some guidance and people that can even physically assist. Most importantly, find a good partner.

I like to think that my kids don't see differences like maybe some other kids do. I'm proud of that. They go to public school. They see people with disabilities in the school and in their classes. Our kids are exposed to that kind of stuff. I even have to tamp it down with Micah because he gets a little too passionate about things.

What we expect out of women versus men in terms of parenting is totally not fair and one hundred percent sexist. We tend to see gender roles in marriage and parenting as the woman does the heavy lifting all the time. I think people assume that if a mother has a significant disability, she is not going to be able to keep up with the child or the child can suffer in some way. I love how people that are not in a situation always have an opinion about it and have already figured it out.

At first, kids are not old enough to understand your disability or why you have it. By the time they are old enough to understand, they've already gotten used to it. All that stuff sort of happens organically. You end up never having a real conversation about it. Society kind of asks those questions for them, and then they come to you and you're forced to deal with the answers. I think that can probably be true with anything -

society dictates what your kids end up wanting to know. The availability of information nowadays is so crazy. Honestly, Micah could go upstairs right now, Google something about my injury and he would get more information than I could give him.

I did have to address it with my oldest at some point; what happened to me, why I am in a chair. He was beginning to realize that the world saw me as different. He was getting questions; what's wrong with you dad, why can't he play baseball, can he hug you, I am not sure of all the questions he was getting. So yes, we have conversations about it, but I also think that it's very important to say we're all different. Everybody has some type of ability or disability or something that makes them different. And that's what's good about the world. I tell him, "You just got lucky you got me, man."

I would consider having another child. I don't like the pregnancy part though. That's the scary part. I would love to adopt and we have talked about doing that somewhere down the road. So much falls on Jess. I've tried to ease the load with attendant care and stuff over the years. She's not my nurse. As the kids get older, I do miss the little rumble monsters around the house. We just got a dog. That will have to do for now.

We have a swing in our backyard. One day, Micah and Bryce were playing on the swing. Jess and I were in the kitchen. Micah was supposed to be watching his younger brother. We heard this blood-curdling scream. Micah runs into the house. He doesn't even say a word, he just runs upstairs and we're like, holy shit, is Bryce dead? Micah didn't tell us what happened or anything. We go outside and Bryce is lying on the ground. He's got a scratch from above his right eye halfway down his cheek. It's a big, long strawberry. That's what we used to call them when we were kids. Jess picks him up and he's just screaming and screaming. We're like, oh my God, is he okay? But he calms down pretty quick. He just handles that sort of thing well. After it became obvious he was going to be fine, I went back and looked at the video. We have a camera that shows that area of the house and the backyard. I watched as he falls off the swing face-first with his eye hitting the ground. His body flips over and his neck goes backwards, like 90 degrees. I almost threw up. If I had seen that happen in real time, I would have wanted to rush him to the emergency room. Fortunately, they are like jello at that age. Welcome to parenting!

*   *   *   *

My father, the father who raised me, the father who fought for me, the father who waged war against racial injustice and discrimination of any kind, finds himself now in the beginning stages of dementia. He is having trouble remembering things. It is hard for him to focus on a conversation. He is becoming easily confused. I just hope I am half the father to my boys that he has been to me.

Chapter 4

Norb
"They're great kids"

Norb with his wife, Barbara, daughter, Jennifer, and son, Matt.

I was among the first of the "Baby Boomers," born in 1946 in Cleveland, Ohio. My father was a veteran. When I was born, he was a truck driver, spending a lot of time on the road. Since I was born with cerebral palsy, although it wasn't called that at the time, he decided he needed to be at home more and used his veteran's preference to become a mail carrier. He ended up loving the job. His veteran benefits also helped me a lot, purchasing such things as special shoes and braces when I was growing up.

My parents were told I would never walk or talk. When I was very young, I lived in a home for children with disabilities ages two to four for a couple of years where I learned how to do both. Braces from waist to heel enabled me to walk.

I was extremely lucky that my parents had high expectations for me. If I wanted something, they always made me ask for it. I had to try to speak. They wanted me talking. I went to a "special" school for children with disabilities through the ninth grade. I received education and various therapies. The school and my parents pushed and challenged me. I was lucky that I lived in Cleveland.

When I reached high school age, I went to a regular public school. My local high school was only a couple of blocks away from my home, but the school system agreed to send me to another high school that was further away. It was more accessible for me and had an adapted gym class. I would fall a lot, but otherwise I managed very well. I had many friends. I got a car when I was old enough so I could go to the school's football and basketball games. I graduated without problems.

After high school, I went to community college. My college expenses were financed almost entirely by vocational rehabilitation services. I initially majored in social work, planning to get a job with the state. I ended up with a degree in therapeutic recreation. I graduated from college in five years.

I was offered a job for one summer as director of a camp for kids with disabilities in Indiana. It changed my life. It was there where I met my future wife, Barbara. She majored in Special Education. She was from Kentucky. After the summer was over, I would drive five to six hours one way to see her. That got old quick, so I decided to move to Lexington.

We married in 1973. We planned to have children, but we waited for a few years to see how things would work with my disability. Of course, with cerebral palsy, there was not an inherited factor involved, but her parents were sure I would have a child with a disability. After five years of marriage, we had a healthy baby girl, Jennifer. We wanted to have two children, but, despite our efforts, it was another five years before our son, Matt, was born.

I don't think my disability greatly impacted my ability to be a parent to my children. I tried to never put myself in a position to do something that I was not capable of doing. I never put them in any danger.

I was very involved with both of my children. I changed diapers. I helped with baths, although that could be a little tricky on occasion. Not long after my daughter was born, I discovered that she seemed to like the way I walked. I would hold her and walk back and forth in the room and she would quickly fall asleep. Obviously, I couldn't chase after my children. I remember an incident when my son first learned to ride his bike. He asked if he could go visit a friend and I let him. He was gone a long time and I began to panic. I went looking for him. He had just stayed away too long at his friend's house, but I told him not to do it again. I would think just about any parent would have a story like that.

I was the manager once of my son's first baseball team. Actually, I volunteered to help in any way I could, thinking I could be a scorekeeper or something, but I was drafted into being the manager. That's what I got for volunteering. I had a talk with the team and the parents about my limitations. A couple of the fathers stepped up and helped me greatly with things I was unable to do, such as pitching batting practice. We finished in second place in the league, missing first place by a single run. My son played soccer, too, but that was a new sport to me. I went to all the practices and games. They won the state championship in the team's second year. My daughter was more the scholastic type and I assisted with her studies. I tried to be involved in much as possible with my kids' lives, although there were times Matt would have liked for me to be less involved.

My role in the family evolved into that of disciplinarian, when one was necessary. I was often the 'heavy,' stepping in when there were problems, setting boundaries and bringing them back when they went out-of-bounds. Matt, for instance, had some problems in high school. If we got a call from the school, I was the one who handled the problem.

They are great kids! They are doing quite well today. Jenny works with an international consulting firm, based in Chicago, with business all over the world, although she works from her home in Lexington. She and her husband have given us two grandchildren, Melina, who is four, and Maya, who is one. Matt works on the tall windmills that generate electrical power. He is a troubleshooter for electrical problems they might have. At the time of this writing, he is working on site in Texas and will move on to Iowa next. Obviously, height doesn't bother him at all. Using his woodworking skills, Matt has made my home extremely accessible.

My daughter lives within a mile of us. I use a walker in the house and a scooter when I am away from home. She is always available if I need her. My wife, Barb, and both of my children help me stay as independent as possible.

Chapter 5

Lee
High School Sweethearts

About six months after I graduated from high school, I was in my car a mile from my house, coming off of a bridge, and was in a head-on accident. I broke my neck and became paralyzed, a C-5 quadriplegic. I spent about three and a half months at a rehabilitation center in Louisville receiving physical and occupational therapy. I thought all I had to do was get out of the rehab center and everything would be great. When I came home, I soon realized that it was not going to be that way. My parents' home, like most any other house at that time and even today, was not accessible. My hospital bed was in the living room because my bedroom was upstairs. The bathroom was not accessible. It was just very difficult.

At the time, my girlfriend, my future wife, was a senior in high school. She would go to school every day and then come to my house to help care for me and to spend as much time with me as she could. My parents learned to adjust to taking care of me and I was trying to learn to be a person with a disability. I was very, very frustrated because I had grown up on a farm and I had been very active, physically fit and loved playing sports. Going through school, I played football and baseball, lifted weights and exercised. I was used to being active and doing things myself. Before my accident, I was attending a local technical institute working on an associate's degree in AutoCAD. I liked carpentry and construction work. I had taken drafting in high school and my plan was to be a builder, designing and building homes.

After my accident, I quickly realized that I could not do that anymore and did not really know what I was going to be able to do. I was still going through physical and occupational therapy at home and my girlfriend was ready to start college. She was planning to go to St. Catherine's, a small Catholic college nearby, after she graduated from high school. She told me, "Well, you can't just sit around here and do nothing with your life. You need to go to college." I was not very keen on that idea because I did not know how I could do it at that time. I was more limited than I am now because I had not learned to adjust to life yet. I still could not write to take notes or take tests. I just did not know how I was going to be able to go to college. She said, "Well, I love you. I'll stay with you, but I'm going off to college and you can either come with me or you can stay home with your Mom and Dad." After hearing that, I was more motivated to go to college.

I had to rethink things. Okay, maybe this is possible. I contacted a vocational rehabilitation counselor. I had exposure to vocational rehabilitation (VR) when I was at the rehab center. A psychologist used to come and talk to me. He would tell me that even though I was paralyzed, I could still live independently. I could still go to work, go to college, and so on. I was not ready for that message while I was in rehab because I was dealing with trying to adjust to having a disability. He scheduled a vocational rehabilitation counselor to come in and speak to me about going to college. At the time, I still had the halo brace on to keep my spine stable while it healed and I had braces on my arms. I could not feed myself and he was talking about how VR could help me go to college. I listened to him for a short time and then I told him, "Listen, buddy, I'm paralyzed. I can't feed myself. I can't dress myself. I can't go to the bathroom by myself. There is no way I am going to college or to work. Thank you for coming in here, but you just need to get out. I'm never going to do that." Fast forward several months later and I am thinking, well, maybe I need to try this college thing.

So, I contacted the local vocational rehabilitation counselor and got things set up. I went to St. Catherine and took nine hours of classes. I did not take 12 hours, which is full-time, because I was not sure if I could handle going to college or not. My girlfriend would drive me there. I used a tape recorder in my classes and for my tests because I still could not write. I ended up doing well with those initial classes and I spoke to my counselor about going to the University of Kentucky (UK) because, at that time, VR had a program there that provided attendant care for students with disabilities who needed it. My girlfriend and I ended up transferring.

When I was at UK, the guys using wheelchairs stayed in one wing of a dorm and the females using wheelchairs stayed in another. I was around some guys that had been paralyzed a few years earlier than I had that were close to my age. They had had time to adjust to their disabilities. I saw them going out and doing things that I did not think I could do. They had assistive technology devices they would use. They showed me a type of writing brace that helped them write. One of the guys had a van that was modified for him to drive. He explained how it worked, showed me the hand controls, and told me that VR helped him pay for the hand controls. I knew that was expensive and I did not have the money to pay for it. One of my concerns about going to work was being able to have a way to get myself there. I was starting to see how I might be able to do things.

First time we went out to the dining hall to eat, I ordered a hamburger. At that time, I would get my girlfriend to feed me. The other guys were eating their hamburgers with their hands. They saw her feeding me and they looked at her and said, "You don't need to feed him. He can feed himself." Whenever I was at home, I did not like trying to feed myself a sandwich because I had a hard time holding it. I would drop the sandwich and get it all over me. When the guys started teasing me about not being able to do something, I saw then I did not have any excuse. It took a little time and trial and error. I had trouble for a little while but over time, I figured out how I could do things. Being around other people with disabilities helped me see that there were things I could do.

I ended up graduating from UK with a degree in Health Administration and my wife received a double major in Math and Computer Science. I went on to graduate school at Eastern Kentucky University (EKU) and got a Master's in Public Administration with a focus on Community Health Administration. When I first got to EKU, there were no accessible apartments. The Disability Coordinator at the college had obtained some grant money to renovate one of the apartments on campus to make it accessible for me. I was able to let them know what I needed to help make the apartment accessible. While I was there going to graduate school, I did an internship with a nursing home company. When I graduated, I got my license as a nursing home administrator.

After graduation, I was an administrator at a nursing home for two years. It was great to have a job where I could support myself and I had health insurance. We were married right after graduation as well. I was fortunate to get a lot of valuable experience doing that job, but I decided that long-term care was not something I wanted to do for the rest of my life. My college undergraduate internship was at a pediatric hospital and I liked working in the pediatric setting. I started looking for a job with the intention of making a transition back to pediatrics and ended up getting a job working for an agency that provides medical services for children with special health care needs. We moved to Louisville and have been there ever since.

My wife and I laugh and say we that we grew up together because we started dating in high school. After I graduated high school, she and my family had to make major adjustments because of my injury. One of the things I remember dealing with was my bedroom was also the living room. My parents are wonderful, great parents, but it was a strain on all of us. I have two younger brothers and sleeping in the living room was just not optimal. My parents were taking care of me, I was trying to be independent, and my girlfriend and I wanted to be able to go places like we used to do. When I moved to UK and got out of the house, it was good for all of us. My parents were still worried about me, but they were glad for me to have that opportunity.

Now fast forward several years, my wife and I have graduated college, we both have jobs and we have a home. I came home from work one day and my wife told me "Well, we're expecting a child." First, I was excited. However, as a person with a disability, I had this fear of, oh Lord, how am I going to take care of a baby? How am I going to assist my wife and help her since I physically cannot do many of the things that other dads do? Again, I was both excited and proud to be a father yet also nervous and worried about what was going to happen. Like any parent, I also worried about having a healthy baby.

My disability was not the biggest concern with us in deciding to have a child. I was concerned about my wife being able to do everything during her pregnancy. One of the things with me being a C-5 quadriplegic; my wife had to do a lot of my personal care. I am fine when I am in up in my wheelchair for the day. I can brush my teeth and that sort of thing, but as far as getting in and out of bed and getting dressed, my wife has to help me. I am blessed and appreciate everything my wife does for me. Well, she still did everything for me up until the last few weeks before her due date. They told her she could only lift a certain amount. One additional blessing is having good, loving, supportive parents. My father would often come to our house, spend the night to give my wife a break periodically, and he still does that now. He came to our house and lived with us for about the last two weeks of her pregnancy. He was there in the mornings to help me and he got me ready for bed at night. He stayed for six weeks following the birth of our baby until my wife got to where she could do what she needed to do for both my daughter and me. My Mom, who was still working (my father was retired), would also come on the weekends since they only lived about an hour away.

When we were at the hospital after my wife gave birth, I could not stay all night and sleep sitting in my wheelchair. I went home so I could sleep in a bed and came back the next day. I remember that bothered me not being able to stay during the night, but I think my wife was glad to have some "alone time" to rest from giving birth. When we left the hospital for good, my parents came along to help with packing all the baby stuff. We put our daughter in the car seat, and I remember looking in the rearview mirror, seeing this little pink hat and I was thinking, "Oh, Lord, this is really happening now."

Since I was not able to do some of the physical things to care for our daughter, I began trying to find other ways of being able to help. When she was a baby and still taking a bottle, there would be some nights that my wife would just be exhausted, especially after she had returned to work, and I would tell her to put the baby beside me so I could feed her. Obviously, I couldn't walk around with our daughter, but I could lay my arm up beside me and prop a pillow around it and my wife would set my daughter in my arm. She would give her the bottle and I could put my hand on the bottle. My daughter could eat until she went to sleep. That was a way for me to be able to feed her in the middle of the night.

Kids are adaptable. We figured a way early on that I could get her out of her crib. When she could stand holding on to the side of the crib, I would lean over the rail, put my arm around her bottom and help her crawl up over into my lap. This way I could get her out of the crib by myself. When she started walking around as a toddler, she would want to sit in my lap, but I could not pick her up by myself. I taught her how to take her foot and step on the frame of my wheelchair. I would hook one arm on the back of my chair, then lean over and put my other arm around her to pull her up until she was strong enough to pull herself up.

When she was just a baby and still bottle feeding, my wife found this device like a sling that you could lay a baby in. We hooked the strap around the back hook of my wheelchair. I could roll around with her without any fear of dropping her. I could bottle feed her in that sling and ride around with her so she would sleep. If we were out in public shopping or something, it was a way that I could carry her.

One challenge was that I could not latch the seatbelt for my daughter. I could unbuckle the seat belt to get her out of the car seat, but I just could not latch it. This was problematic if I wanted to pick her up from daycare, for instance. The staff at the daycare was willing to accommodate me with this issue. When I picked her up, the daycare staff would come out and buckle her in until she was big enough to buckle herself. If we had a problem on the way home, I could get her out on my own. I just could not latch her in by myself.

When my daughter would transition to different school groups or sports programs, parents and coaches were very welcoming to me. Sometimes, however, people would want to go out after a game or team function for a group dinner and not realize that I could not get into a certain area of the restaurant. I quickly learned to ask about accessibility if going to a new place. You learn to be proactive about that sort of thing. In addition, after they knew to ask about it, the other parents would just ask about accessibility when picking a place for all of us to eat.

We have done a lot of traveling with our daughter for her sports. A lot of accessible hotel rooms only have a king bed to make more space in the room which is great for the person with the disability; but once you start traveling with a kid, particularly when that kid is a teenager, that does not work. We would try to always ask for an accessible room with double beds, but, if not, we would ask for a roll away bed.

I mentioned I played sports in high school. I played baseball and football. My daughter loved sports from an early age and I loved being involved in her sports. When she started playing coach-pitch baseball, I would get out in the backyard with her and practice with her so she could hit the ball. She quickly got tired of collecting all the balls she hit if my wife was not there to get them. Not to mention, I had to be close to her when I pitched and I could not get out of the way of a ball coming at me, increasing the likelihood of me being hit. My fingers on my right hand were tight enough that I could hold the ball in my hand so I could grasp it. I could sit back from her and throw underhand for her to hit it. I got fairly good at it, but I do not have a lot of strength. I had to sit about 10 or 12 feet from her. The balls were not as hard as real baseballs, but they were hard enough. Even then, she was very athletic, very good at sports. Soon she was hitting the ball hard, and sometimes the ball would hit me. As a result, I was getting bruises. We switched to a tennis ball, but even that stings. I ended up putting metal lawn chairs in front of me as a blockade. I would pitch the ball and then duck in behind the lawn chair. When she hit it, it would hit the lawn chair instead of me. She still did not like having to go run down all the balls by herself.

I looked around and came across a device that was used to practice hitting. It had two strings through the center of a ball and a hook on the end of it. It had two handles. I could take it, tie the end of it to a post I would get back and pull the handles and it would zip the ball down to her to hit it. I would hold the handles apart and the ball would stop right before it would hit me. That worked really well. She could hit the ball, but it would not hit me. I could send it back to her and she did not have to go chase any balls.

We have been to the beach a few times. I bought a beach umbrella that has sides on it. We would take the umbrella when we would go to the beach and put it around me. Some public beaches have balloon tire beach chairs and we have used those a few times so that I could go sit on the beach and watch my wife and daughter in the ocean. When we go, we usually try to find a hotel with a nice boardwalk or a huge deck that comes out so that I can sit on the deck and watch. If I get hot, I can just go back inside and cool down.

As a young child before she first went to school, my disability was just natural for my daughter. She had no reason to think our family was different. When she started school, particularly kindergarten and particularly with younger kids, my disability got attention. Kids are naturally inquisitive. The question I would get sometimes when we were first around some new kids would be: why are you in a wheelchair? Or why don't your legs work? I would explain to the kids about being in a car accident and becoming paralyzed and 'that's why you should always wear your seat belt.' Usually that would suffice and they would move on. I would get the question a couple of times and then they did not pay attention to it. However, there would be times when I would have that one kid that would keep coming back and asking the same question every time he saw me. My daughter would get frustrated. She would not really say anything until we were in the car or at home. Then she would say, "I don't know why that kid asked you that question. It is obvious why you are in a wheelchair. You have a disability." She had grown up with me like this her whole life. I would say, "Well, you know, he's a kid. He is not used to it and does not see it much. He'll get used to it over time." Usually, the kid would quit asking the question. Going to school does make a difference. Kids really do not see differences until they go to school and people start pointing it out.

I'm not saying there would not be times it would bother her to go somewhere and we could not do certain things because it was not accessible, but she adapted to that and did not let it stop her from wanting to go do things with me. That is the way it has always been and it has never bothered her for me to be around her friends or anything like that. I work, I like sports and I am involved in things. I am not different from anybody else except for the fact I use a wheelchair.

Do not get me wrong, it is not that I have not also gotten frustrated about some things. Like, if I cannot get in somewhere because maybe there is not a curb cut, or a ramp. Or, I could not get up close to something like a table that is too high, but you cannot let your frustration keep you from going and doing things. Also, those type of things did not happen that often. Plus, if you talk to people, most of the time they are willing to make adjustments. When my daughter was in elementary school and was playing volleyball, one of the schools where she played had a gym on the second floor of an old church. There was no elevator. We arrived there and I could not get in to watch her play. I did not make a big deal out of it. I just told my wife and daughter to go on in. After it was over, I contacted the athletic director at her school and said, "I could not get into to see her play. That gym is not accessible." From then on, when she was scheduled to play against that school, either they came to our gym or the match was scheduled at another school with a gym on the ground floor. Every year after that at the beginning of the season I would remind them to make sure the team was not scheduled to play in that gym. They always accommodated me.

I do not think a person should let their fear of having a disability stop them from being a parent if that is what they want to do. There are ways to adapt. Do not get caught up on how you physically cannot do this or that. The main thing is just to be there, be involved with your child, go to parent teacher conferences, go to ball games, go places with your child and their friends and participate in activities because just being involved in your child's life shows them that you love them and you care about them. Whether you have a disability or not you can be involved and show your child and your family that you love them.

Our daughter is a freshman in college now. My wife and I are very proud of her. I appreciate all the love and support my wife has given to me and to our family over the years.

Chapter 6
Donna
May 5th Miracles

Donna and her sons

Brandon and Matthew

According to the Webster's Dictionary, a miracle is defined as:

1. an *extraordinary event* manifesting divine intervention in human affairs;
2. an extremely *outstanding* or unusual event, thing, or *accomplishment;*
3. a *divinely natural phenomenon* experienced humanly as the fulfillment of spiritual law (according to the Christian Science Monitor).

Extraordinary event? You better believe it.

Outstanding accomplishment? Most definitely.

Divine phenomenon? In so many ways.

My sons, Matthew and Brandon are my definitions for the word miracle. On May 5th of 1991, my first miracle arrived. He was six weeks early and tiny, but he was beautiful. My second miracle arrived on May 5th of 1995 when I gave birth to my second son. What a beautiful surprise this little miracle was when he arrived. Babies are born every second and they are each and every one a miracle. Maybe I am a bit biased, but I really do believe that my babies are more miraculous than most.

I was informed seven years prior to my first pregnancy that having children was out of the question for "someone like me." At the age of 18, I asked my then-gynecologist if he could prescribe me birth control pills and rather than answer my question, he asked me a question. I was asked, "why do you want them?" The obvious answer was I did not want to get pregnant, but I suppose since having a physical disability (juvenile rheumatoid arthritis) since age 4, my doctor felt (and indicated to me) I did not need them.

It was a common opinion. I would not date, get married or have or need children. My family, friends, and now my healthcare providers seemed to align with this thinking and sadly, this was not the first time I had heard a physician make a similar statement. At age 15, I vividly recall my doctor speaking to my parents about my future. According to him, it would not include dating, marriage, college, career, or kids. My parents were instructed to apply for disability and let me live as comfortably as possible. Although I had a boyfriend at the time, I let these thoughts and these words of my doctors bury deep in my thoughts and take up residence.

After this heartbreaking conversation filled with complete negativity, I was left believing I should not date, could not date and would never be able to conceive. I was informed if my body should ever permit a pregnancy, I would not see the pregnancy through to fruition. Over the next several years, I played a not so convincing game of sour grapes. I tried with little success to convince myself that I did not really want children. I asked myself, why would I want to bring innocent children into my messed up, unsure, and chaotic life. I was convinced I could not be a good parent because I had a disability.

I have rheumatoid arthritis in every joint. From my jaw to my toes. My body is distorted and seriously deformed from juvenile arthritis and my range of motion and physical ability are limited. I endure daily pain, sometimes severe, a lack of mobility and many other hardships that my arthritis has dumped on me. However, prior to this conversation with one doctor, I always felt I was like everyone else and never saw myself as he described, "crippled", "different", or "unable". Was I fooling myself? Was I living in a make-believe world? Maybe avoiding mirrors and hiding my hands should have clued me in. Maybe I really was "different and not able". I had never seen it. I was just me, a simple person who loved life, I was Donna. I was fun, friendly and capable of receiving and giving love. I was me and I wanted to do everything my peers were doing.

AND....I did! I fell in love. I got engaged.

AND I got pregnant!

Oh my gosh! Pregnant? What? How? This was not supposed to happen to "someone like me".

BUT, it was true, I was pregnant. How was that even possible? Were the results correct? I tested again, several times, just to confirm that the impossible was possible and I was going to have a BABY!

I was afraid to show my excitement, share my amazing news and plan my mommy-hood future. I kept hearing the message, "if you ever get pregnant you will not carry a baby to term, you will miscarry, your body will not tolerate a pregnancy. In the event you do conceive and carry to term, you cannot physically, financially, and emotionally raise a child." I kept hearing it, but I refused to believe it.

I was pregnant! I was carrying an amazing gift inside of me, I would be a good Mommy and I WOULD HAVE THIS BABY. I knew my baby was due on June 19th, 1991 so when I felt the horrible pain from cramping and saw the blood on April 3rd, I was nervous. I was so afraid. The doctor told me this would happen.

I begged my god. I prayed so hard. I continued to refuse to believe the doctor and turned the words away.

I KNEW DIFFERENT! I was going to give birth and this day was not the day. After an emergency room visit, I was sent home, placed on bed rest and given medication to stop my contractions. I was never so good to my body. I rested as instructed and believed with every fiber in my body that I would soon hold a baby in my arms.

The day was May 5th, 1991 (it was my mothers' birthday). I felt my stomach tighten. It was contractions again, but this time my water broke and there was no more halting my labor. I was taken to the emergency room, sent to the labor and delivery unit and four hours later witnessed a real miracle.

I felt little pain. I felt only love, happiness and pure joy. At only five pounds and two ounces and measuring less than eighteen inches, my baby boy was really here and laying swaddled in my arms. I could have never imagined this feeling. Holding your baby in your arms for the first time is a feeling one cannot adequately describe. With so much emotion, I vowed I would be the best Mommy I could be.

When Matthew was only four months old, I became a single parent and now I vowed I would be the best Mommy and Daddy I could ever be. No pain, no deformity, no limited mobility, no rude comments from people passing, no opinions of others... NOTHING would stop me from showing my precious gift what babies need most, LOVE!

Love was the easy part. I was very concerned about taking care of this little human. Up to that point, I had proven everybody wrong: I could go to college, I could go to work, I could get a fiancé, I could have a baby. I had learned adaptations from an early age. I knew if one thing didn't work, I would try something else. This adaptability was really tested when I became a parent. Interestingly enough, I think the majority of people with physical disabilities, I say this all the time, are the most creative people on the planet because we have to adapt, be creative and learn what works for us. There were a lot of learning curves that came with raising a baby.

Feeding a baby. That is simple. But, one problem was as simple as opening a baby bottle. With my hands the way they are, it is hard to grip anything. I had learned to use all types of jar openers and devices, but the one thing that wasn't on the market was a baby bottle opener. Pliers and vice grips serve many purposes. I had to find things that worked for me. It took a lot of creativity. Disposable diapers today have Velcro, but 30 years ago they only had tape and that that tape was some seriously strong adhesive. I kept a pair of scissors by the crib to help me with the tape. I wouldn't recommend that as an ideal parenting practice, but I had to do what worked for me and to keep my baby fresh and clean. Baby clothes. Easy stuff, right? Not so much. Clothes were very difficult. Zippers and snaps were doable, but not buttons. I would sew Velcro into my son's baby clothes.

At the time, there wasn't a lot of assistive technology around to help. You had to make your own if you needed it. Car seats, also known as nightmares! I had to use a screwdriver with duct tape on the end to press the release button on the car seat. Every time I used it, I prayed that it worked. It just meant more adapting and more creativity and figuring out what was going to work.

These are just some of the things that I think individuals who have a disability and are thinking about parenthood have to consider. These are some of the things we're up against. A lot of people just take it for granted, you're going to have a baby, you can do the bottles, you can do the diapers, you can unpack the stroller, do the car seats, and you don't think that much about it.

My creative skills kicked into high gear and I made many accommodations for the daily tasks associated with raising an infant, toddler, and child. Opting for Playtex bottles (with bags) for ease of use. Sometimes needing scissors to cut the extra adhesive tape when changing disposable diapers. Pushing my son(s) through the house in the stroller when I could not carry them. Teaching them to hug my neck to ease the process of picking them up. If I needed help living on my own as a single mom, I would occasionally tap my ceiling with a broom handle to alert my upstairs neighbors that I could use a little help. There was never any shame or embarrassment, only love, acceptance, and pride.

Although I did many things differently, I was confused when I learned I had been turned into Child Protective Services (CPS). Apparently, a complete stranger, after seeing me in public with my 2-year-old son, thought I would be unfit because, according to them, I could barely function. Fortunately for my son and me, Child CPS saw it differently. Often, children with parents who have disabilities are removed from their home. I was blessed that after two visits to my home and interviewing people who knew me and my circumstances, CPS ruled in my favor.

Life was amazing with my toddler son. Days were full of fun, playing in parks, learning to swim and being the cheering mom at T-ball. But, I wanted and needed adult company. Maybe, I should seek a social life, maybe even date again. So, I did date again and this time, I opted for birth control because I can get pregnant and I can give birth.

Birth control would assure me that I would not get pregnant. Or so I thought. I soon found myself seeking an explanation for a missed period. I was so convinced it could not be a pregnancy. I was on BIRTH CONTROL. I waited days, even weeks, to call my obstetrician for an appointment. I then cancelled that appointment, but on my 29th birthday, I made myself call for another appointment and go in for a pregnancy test. I was so sure I was not pregnant. I went to a health clinic, not my physician's office, to learn the reason for that missed period. I knew that, if I should be pregnant; I had to know early in the pregnancy so I could once again halt all medications.

I recall wiping the tears and still hearing the words. YOU ARE PREGNANT!

Oh my gosh! I cannot believe this! How could it be? I was on birth control.

I was excited but scared. I was happy but sad.

This news of my pregnancy was apparently not the news that the father of my baby wanted to hear. Upon my announcing my pregnancy, he was gone. Just like that he removed himself from the scene.

Having been there and done it once, I knew I would be okay. Everything would be fine. My physician had faith that because my first pregnancy went well, this one would as well. I mean, obviously, I could get pregnant and I could also see a pregnancy through to birth so I once again treated my body better than ever and knew I was on my way to a second little miracle.

I truly was blessed until at four months into my pregnancy I got "that" phone call…the results for my alpha fetoprotein test were in and, according to my doctor, they were "not normal". This meant the baby growing inside of me could possibly have some developmental abnormalities. At my doctor's recommendation, I sought the guidance of a specialist in high risk pregnancies and educated myself about Down's Syndrome and other developmental abnormalities so I would be prepared should I need to be. Medical professionals, counselors, friends, and even some family were concerned for me and my ability to parent two children, even more so should this pregnancy result in a child with special healthcare needs.

I was given the option to have an amniocentesis for more conclusive answers, but knowing the dangers of the test, I declined. I was advised that an abortion should be a serious consideration. With this advice, I turned to a dear friend. I remember asking my best friend who had a son with cerebral palsy if she had known her son would require "extra" attention, would she have aborted him? Her response was a resounding NO! I even asked my own Mom, had she been given the choice to "abort" or terminate me upon my diagnosis, would she have elected to do so. She quickly replied she would not have done any such thing. After the consultation and watching the amniocentesis video, and with fear attempting to take me over, I recall walking across the doctors' parking lot and looking up at the sky for answers. I am not sure what, where or why, but, before I reached the car, I knew I would see my pregnancy to term and that no matter what, Matthew, my soon-to-be-second baby boy, and I, would be fine.

For the next four months, I prepared Matthew to be a big brother. We attended big brother classes, toured the hospital and decorated our new house for his little brother's arrival. I waited patiently. I wondered many of those long days and sleepless nights if my baby boy would be okay. I remained faithful that no matter what, we – he, Matthew and I – would be just fine.

Once again, it was May 5th, but the year was 1995. I felt "those" familiar pains. The same as I felt on May 5th, 1991. I thought to myself, it could not be labor, I still had 10 days before my due date and the odds of having my baby on his brother's and his grandmother's birthday seemed unthinkable. I called my Mom at work and told her I was in labor and, like me, she said there was no way. She said I was just excited with anticipation because everyone had said for nine months, I could possibly have both of my babies on her birthday. I said "fine" and waited for only a few minutes and then the pain came again and again. I told Mom I have to get to the hospital NOW! She drove home, picked Matthew and me up, and before long we were in the Emergency Room where I was admitted, but instructed it may be after midnight before I gave birth.

With this news, my Mom took Matthew to the hospital cafeteria to get dinner. My pains grew worse, so I called for the nurse. The nurse did an examination and nervously called down the hallway for help, making it clear that she needed a doctor. I KNEW IT WAS TIME and within minutes and before my Mom and Matthew returned from the cafeteria, I had given birth via natural delivery. Brandon was a healthy, 6lb 11oz, 21-inch, beautiful baby boy! I once again held a tiny miracle, my son and Matthew's baby brother.

I was clearly starting all over with the bottles and the diapers and all those things that babies need. But my four-year-old knew (children are resilient, adaptable, and very smart), that sometimes Mommy needed help with his baby brother.

When my boys were seven and three, my oldest started to ask me questions. He was in school and was learning his Mom was not like the other mommies. I set both of my boys down and explained to them in seven-year-old and three-year-old terminology what was "up with Mom" and what made Mom different. Honestly, that conversation did so much. It was so positive. It took a lot off my shoulders. I was always so worried and scared about not only what they were going to think, but what their friends in school might say. Would they have to deal with their friends teasing them? Once I had that conversation and they knew this was something Mom had no control over, I (and they) felt a lot better.

It was not always easy, but it was always worth it. The thousands of comments from strangers. Your brothers are so cute. Do you babysit them? Are you their aunt? How did you adopt? YOU had children? I have heard it all and seen even more. The looks cannot be avoided. Having your young sons defend you to complete strangers. Wiping their tears when other kids tease them because of their "monster" Mom. Watching them learn compassion and empathy was amazing. They cared for others then as they do today.

By choice, I remained a single Mom. My sons did not grow up with a male role model in the home so I entered them in the YMCA sports programs where they would at least have (some) male role models. My oldest was once on a soccer team that was going to have a parent-child soccer game. I wanted to participate. Matthew asked me, "Mom, how are you going to do that?" I said "I can be goalie, I won't have to move much." I started the game at goalie. I wasn't very good. The other team scored a lot. I couldn't catch a ball if my life depended upon it. I certainly couldn't get on the ground. It was hilarious because everyone knew that was going to happen. The kids and everybody were great about it. I only played goalie for a small part of the game. I think that everyone got a lesson in inclusion that day.

One of the things I say a lot, especially to individuals with disabilities who are considering becoming parents and worried about how they are going to teach their son or daughter: your children will teach you as much as you teach them. I mean that 100%. You won't even think about that until you're actually going through it. Your children are learning and absorbing all the time.

I tried very hard never to put my children in a position to have to help me. If they saw me struggling, I never wanted them to think that Mom needed them. I didn't want to put that kind of pressure on them. As they got older and they would want to go stay all night with their friends, I didn't want them to think they had to stay home because of Mom's needs. I didn't want to ever have to deal with that. I let them learn on their own when to help. They learned to say "Mom, let me help you with that." My disability became as much a part of their lifestyle as it was of mine. We always had a lot of their friends around the house and I've had many of them say, "I hope you're not offended when I say this, but being around you taught me a lot."

Matthew and Brandon learned a lot by observing and it's taught them to be accepting and respectful of people and their differences. Now, I am a Grammy and so proud. I never imagined the day when I would see myself as a grandma! Now, my grandkids are learning to adapt to me. "Grammy, let me try." If I can't do something, they want to help me. We try to open and do many things together. Sometimes we get it and sometimes we don't. I teach them that sometimes things just don't work. Sometimes the hands just don't do what they're supposed to do, and that's okay. In an odd sort of way, having a person with a disability around children teaches them lessons they won't learn anywhere else. You have to expose yourself to children and let them know you're vulnerable. We all are. There are a lot of lessons that can be learned from that.

There is no rule book for raising children. When my first son was born, there was a group called the Rockin' Grannies that would come to the nursery. One of them would come and talk with me. She told me "Honey, they (babies) come with rules written all over them, but the rules get washed off with their first bath." The rules are going to change. My children and I had to learn as we went along.

Society still doesn't accept or expect people with disabilities as parents. When I was raising my boys, I don't know how many times I was called the babysitter or the aunt or the neighbor. So many people said to me with obvious surprise and a touch of disdain, 'Oh, you had kids?' I was asked by medical professionals why I wanted to have children. I heard 'why would you want to do that to a child?' Even though my children are now adults, I know the bias against parents with disabilities, particularly against parents with intellectual disabilities, remains strong.

Why should I be less entitled to have children than anyone else? A physically healthy family does not necessarily translate to a good family. Not everyone is capable of being a good parent, but a disability has little to do with it. Individuals need to ask themselves if they really want to have children. What is their experience with children? Have they spent time with a small child? Have they done any babysitting? Prospective parents with disabilities may have a few more questions to ask. Are they physically capable and healthy enough to become pregnant? Can you physically handle raising children and do you have the support you need?

Have I ever advised people against having children? I have. I have spoken to many people with and without disabilities about parenting. The first thing I tell them is, it's hard to be a parent. Can you take care of a child and if you can't take care of them on your own, are you going to have a strong enough support system to help? There are a lot of little things that you don't think about. They're going to get hurt. Are you going to be able to pick them up off the floor in time to keep them from choking? This applies to all parents. I think a person has to be self-aware. I once had a couple come to me. They were both individuals with cerebral palsy, both wheelchair users who wanted to have a child and their concern was: would this be fair to their child? That's not even a fair question. To me, there are many other questions. Are you going to be prepared to talk to your child about your disability? Why can't you do some of the things that your friend's parents can do? And so many more. If they don't have the support system and they don't feel prepared to have those conversations, then I've invited them to revisit the idea of becoming a parent.

I feel extremely blessed to have had children. I wouldn't want to take that feeling from any potential parent. It has to be the person's decision – not the doctor, friend, or a family member. The important thing is to know you can provide, you can be loving, supportive and nurturing. If you have those abilities, everything else can be worked out.

On May 5th, 2021 my miracles, my tiny babies turned 30 and 26 and I simply stare in amazement at the men they have become. We have had our ups, our downs, our curve balls, and our potholes. We have laughed, we have cried, we have been sad, and we have been silly. My boys have seen me endure the pain and the adversities of my arthritis. They have seen me fight my way back from hemolytic anemia and colon cancer. We have lived, we have loved, and we have laughed. They have been scared and so have I, but together we survived

Matthew, Donna and Brandon

Chapter 7

Keith
"Don't fill your head with worries and what ifs"

Keith with his daughter, Kayla, and his wife, Shannon

I am married with a seven-year-old daughter, Kayla. My wife, Shannon, and Kayla are not disabled. I have a family history regarding disability. I have a congenital disability of bilateral severe clubfeet. That's the first thing that I'll list and it is inherited. One of my Dad's brothers, my uncle, also had that condition and one of my Mom's uncle's had it. I also live with general anxiety disorder and major depressive disorder. I have chronic pain due to my clubfeet. These disabilities are all involved in my parenting and in my family interactions.

When my wife and I were talking about having a child, I was not yet diagnosed with my mental health conditions, but I did obviously have clubfeet. I had over a dozen surgeries as a child. I continued to have chronic pain and issues related to the clubfeet. I wear below the knee AFOs (ankle-foot orthotics). The disability was definitely something that went into our decision-making. We discussed it. I researched it. Luckily in the age of social media, I was able to reach out to people with the same disability. I'm a member of a clubfoot Facebook group. I discussed it with some people on the group, asked for some information, found statistics of the likelihood of a parent passing it down. Ultimately, we made the decision that, while we all want our children to be as healthy as possible, to a certain extent my clubfeet made me who I am and I don't feel I turned out to be too bad of a person. Even if our child were to inherit club feet, we would still love her, of course, and do the best by her and give her a good life. It would not be necessarily the most defining thing in her life as it hasn't been in mine.

We had a daughter. I think club feet is more prevalent in boys, but girls can have it. The soccer player, Mia Hamm, was born with club feet, although a much less severe case than mine. I would say she adapted to it pretty well. Nonetheless, our daughter was not born with the condition.

One of my bigger challenges in being a parent as far as my physical disability goes was when my daughter was a toddler who in a running phase. By the time she was, I don't know, three, she could outrun me. I always had a concern if we were in the front yard alone she could take off and I couldn't catch her. Then she went through about a six-monthphase where, in any store we were in, she wanted to be out of the cart and down on the floor. As soon as her feet hit the floor, she took off running. I would tell her, "You can't run, I'm not going to put you down if you are going to run." She would say, "No, I won't run, no, no, no," and then boom, she's gone. When we were at the grocery store or the department store, my wife would be there, too. It only took one or two times of her running and us looking at each other and me saying, "you gotta chase her." It just turned into a routine. She hits the floor and takes off, my wife and I would say, "We've got a runner," and she goes after her. As far as adapting to that, I found that Walgreens is small enough with enough corner mirrors, that I could let her play her game safely and chase her around the store and let her get it out of her system.

My chronic pain offers other challenges that limit my activities. Going to the zoo is a pretty normal thing for a parent to do with their child, but I have extra considerations. I tire easily. I have greater pain the longer I walk or stand. We went to Disney World at New Year's and I ended up renting a scooter. It was probably the best thing I ever did at any park in the world. Since then, I've rented scooters at the zoo which has been nice.

With my mental health, the biggest challenge was when I first started having panic attacks. I didn't know what they were. I thought I was having a stroke and it was happening every couple of days. I didn't know what was going on until I ended up seeing a neurologist and a psychiatrist. It was difficult, because when I had the panic attacks, it affected my entire body and then I would have had a terrible migraine for at least the whole day. I would be incapacitated, there were days where all I could do is lay in bed. This brought on feelings of inferiority and inadequacy that went with not being able to take care of my child and having to rely on my wife to do everything.

But I really should start at the beginning with my mental health. I wasn't diagnosed with a mental illness until my thirties, but I believe I may have had one since I was in high school. Looking back, there were signs from high school through college and in young adulthood. I dismissed it all. "My life's too good to be depressed". "I'm depressed, yeah, but not, like, clinically depressed."

My uncle, who also experiences clinical depression, was the Poet Laureate of his home state. He wrote, "why does man alone get out of bed?" I asked him what he meant by that. He said it's a description of his depression. It was so true for me, but I still didn't make the connection, even in the beginning of college.

I was a cutter briefly in my freshmen year of college. Not many people know that because when I tell people, they get real weird. There's so much stigma around cutting. I think It's important to normalize it. I don't mean normalize doing it, I give it zero out of ten, I would not recommend it. I just mean we shouldn't act like it doesn't happen, or that it always means suicide. It was freshmen year, first semester, and I didn't have many friends. I think I still had undiagnosed depression and I drank. A lot. I cut to feel alive, something... ANYTHING. I wasn't suicidal at all. I never cut again, after that semester.

Speaking of being suicidal... have you ever been suicidal? No? You ever been driving down the road and imagine if you just drove off the edge? High speed on the highway into a ditch? Imagine what the world would be like without you. An escape from pain and suffering. To sleep no more. I thought it was just my overactive imagination. Turns out I may have had "passive" suicidal ideation in my twenties, but I never actually entertained trying to kill myself.

With proper medication and better understanding of my illnesses, I'm doing pretty well now. No panic attacks. Some depression, but not as bad. No cutting. No imaginations of death. I'm not saying have a baby for an extra protective factor. I'm saying that if suicidality is stopping you from having a baby, don't let it. My daughter is my BEST protective factor. She makes me want to take my medicine and be healthy.

I can't say that I faced any specific instances of bias or discrimination as a parent with a disability other than when she was in her running phase and people gave me dirty looks because a little kid was running around in a store, but I think that would probably happen to any parent. My family has always been supportive. My wife certainly picks up the slack when needed. As I mentioned earlier, I'm a member of a group on Facebook of people with club feet. That has been helpful at times. I just try to be my best self, be my healthiest self so that I can be there for my family. I take my medicine for my mental health and I have a leg brace that helps me walk for longer distances and stand for longer periods of time. That improves my quality of life so I can be there for my daughter as much as I can.

Kayla learned early on to adapt to some of my limitations. For example, with my anxieties would come migraine headaches. Unfortunately, anytime I get a headache, it turns into a migraine even if it's not anxiety related. Kayla learned that when we said that Daddy's getting a headache, she had to be quiet. For a four or five-year-old to tone it down, that is kind of unique.

I would tell a person with a disability who is considering parenthood don't fill your head with worries and what ifs. There are certainly people and communities out there that can help with adaptations, accommodations and suggestions. Before becoming a parent, I knew parents who had quadriplegia and parents who had other disabilities. I had that perspective that it could be done. Role modeling was already there for me, but I'm sure there are plenty of people out there that don't have those people in their lives that they've seen do it already. It's like anything else, you read. You research. You rise to the occasion.

It is absolutely more difficult to be a mother with a disability than a father with a disability. Society still has this view that mothers are the primary caretakers. As a father, there's less expected of me, although in our household, we share responsibility. People will question a mother's ability to be a parent more than they will mine. If Shannon and I were taking Kayla into a building, people won't give it a second thought because the mother is there and is able-bodied. Women with disabilities are much more vulnerable to criticism.

As I said earlier, Kayla knew from an early age that when I was getting a headache, she had to be quiet. Even as a little two-year-old or three-year-old walking around just like any other kids, she put my shoes on and walked around being Daddy, even though one has metal bars on it. Like there's nothing to it and she knows that I can't walk as long as other people and I need to take breaks and all that stuff. Then something happened a few months ago that kind of took me back. She is seven now. I said something offhand about having a disability. And she looked at me and said, "Daddy, you don't have a disability." I thought what in the world is this kid thinking. She knows all this. And yet she still didn't connect the word with me. We have made an effort of having inclusive books in the house like a princess in a wheelchair and all this stuff. What she said just blew me away. She seemed to have somehow developed a negative connotation about disability. The word disability to her at that point in time was kind of a bad word. Her Daddy couldn't have one of those. I sat down and I talked to her and I told her of course Daddy has a disability. I wear this leg brace and it helps me. I can do things other people do I just do it differently. I had to kind of address that and turn it upside down and say this isn't a bad thing. It's just that everyone's different. It was really interesting to get that feedback from her. She picked up on the negativity related to disability outside of the home after all those inclusive books and everything else and despite knowing Daddy's friends in wheelchairs. Somehow, society's negative attitudes had penetrated into her way of thinking.

Chapter 8

Nanci
"The best choice
I could ever make"

Nanci with her son, Easton.

I was born in Frankfort, Kentucky, to a single mother on August 21st, 1981, which is also the same birthday of my birth father. My Mom found that kind of ironic and loved that I was born on his birthday because she said he would never forget the day I was born. I find it funny.

My mother and father met in 1979 while working for what was then called the Kentucky Department for Environmental Protection. When my father walked in for his interview, my mother's supervisor told her, "Yes, he's single." She often reminisced about going to Bob Segar concerts with him. She loved Bob Segar as much as she loved him, I would like to imagine. After a few years of dating, my father left my mother, married someone else, and he went on to have two more daughters and a son. My mother was pregnant with me. He now lives in New Mexico and has done pretty well for himself as a college professor. I have established a relationship with him over the years and he has grown on me a bit. I don't know quite what or how to feel now. I was angry for so long for him abandoning Mom and me. It took a toll on my mental health because I felt like it was because of me that my parents weren't together. I should have never been born was my rationale. For her happiness. Later on down the line, Mom told me, "Hell no, that ain't your fault, Nanci!" I know that now, but the damage was already there and it festered over the years.

Sometime in 1984, my mom moved us back to her hometown of Hazard in Eastern Kentucky where I would grow up like she had. Before she left Frankfort, she became pregnant again. That's when my stepfather came into the picture. He was 21 and Mom was 28 and pregnant by another man. But he didn't care because he was smitten with her. He was simply the greatest and their love and respect for each other was immeasurable. His laugh was contagious and he laughed often. He was my Dad who taught me how to drive. He took me under his wing and when my birth father came back into the picture when I was 12, he said, "that's MY baby!" He loved us all so much.

Unfortunately, he passed from Multiple Sclerosis and complications. For the last few years of his life, he didn't recognize any of us. He lost his ability to walk, eat, and even his ability to hug. He was such a positive influence growing up and loved us all beyond reason or doubt. Watching his health slowly deteriorate and the profound images ingrained in my brain affects me to this day. It was a traumatic experience for us all. He lost everything and so did we. We lost our home, his job, friends, and coworkers. But he didn't lose us. Watching those events unfold were very sad. Sad is the only way I know to put it. It affected my mental health greatly during that time, I felt abandoned by God, I felt punished. I felt like it was because of me, AGAIN. I'm the curse. You start to believe the bad after a while when the negative self-talk is loud and obnoxious and clouds your thinking and judgement. I only hoped things would get better as the years went by or just accept this as who I am.

So, I grew up in Hazard and had a great childhood for the most part. I spent time with my Papaw and Granny and had a whole slew of cousins that are still my best friends to this day. I was super close with my aunts and still am. They're my lifeline nowadays. But I remember being in first grade and feeling 'different.' I don't exactly know why and still to this day I don't. I just felt different than the other kids. I was happy but I wasn't. From the time I could remember, I felt anxious all the time. I was hypersensitive to everything and very emotional. I once ran through an entire briar patch in shorts because I had a panic attack and thought I was lost in the woods. My cousins were there and they tried to stop me but they couldn't catch me and weren't about to run through a briar patch behind me. When I got home, my legs had deep scratch marks and burned. I finally felt it. While running I felt nothing. That was my first panic attack. After that my Mom tried to take me to a counselor, but nothing came of it. Stigma is rampant in the hills and we stopped going after one visit.

I didn't know exactly why we went at that time, but I understand now. In grade school I remember having extreme test anxiety. Every morning break, we would come back to class and I would cry and panic because math class was next. I wanted to go home. I felt so sick. In middle school, things were rough, but I imagine they are rough for everyone. I would literally get sick to have to go to school. I had friends, but was picked on during this time. Maybe we all were? Who knows, but it once again affected me. One time in middle school, a classmate told me that I needed to take a bath. As a result, I showered and doused myself in anything with a scent because that one statement affected me on a mental level. High school was different. I had friends that were very close and still are. I started 'dating'. It sucked. I stopped, but the teasing didn't. And so, I pushed through all the teasing and name calling and persevered. I graduated in 1999.

At the age of 18, my nurse practitioner prescribed Prozac to treat depression. At that time, Prozac was a hot ticket item for those suffering from mental illness. It worked for a while but not for long as I stopped taking it. I eventually went on to obtain my degree in Speech Communication with an emphasis in Human Services from Eastern Kentucky University. During my college years, I had several bouts of erratic and reckless behavior, panic attacks, drug and alcohol use, and several bad relationships. I would always date and then have a bad breakup and repeat. Never was I not in a relationship. They were all rocky to say the least.

I would threaten to kill myself several times during my college years, but never acted upon the threats. I became more and more depressed. I would call my Mom crying most every day because I wanted to run away from my emotions and come home. In relationships, I needed that security and hated to be 'alone'. I had abandonment issues since I was little. I was always afraid that people I loved were going to leave me and for the most part, they did. I devoted too much of my time and energy to those who didn't appreciate what I had to offer. In hindsight, I should have focused on my family instead.

Sometime after college, I was officially diagnosed with Bipolar II Disorder. I was on several different medications and became overmedicated. Seroquel, Klonopin, Gabapentin, Abilify, and Lamictal. Seroquel caused me to gain weight and black out. One time I woke up in the middle of my bedroom confused and scared because I lost control of my body and mind. The mental health counselor that I talked to on a regular basis eventually left. I still don't know where my files are to this day. It just went out of business. I stopped taking medication again! I had a bad habit of that.

In 2007, I began cutting in secret. I broke a glass and it became my go to. I felt worthless and stupid and was in so much mental anguish that I just wanted the pain and the intrusive thoughts to stop. Negative self-talk consumed my life and I needed a release. I had known since I was a kid that I didn't feel right. I now believe that those intrusive thoughts were with me for as long as I can remember. The blame I had put on myself was colossal. I couldn't take it anymore, so I slid the glass on my arms and wrists. I hid the marks for weeks from my family and coworkers. I never reached out for help from anyone.

My erratic behavior continued. The alcohol use increased dramatically while my work performance decreased. I was losing it and needed to save myself. During this time, in 2009, I met a man and was married to him for three years before he left me for another woman. Again, abandonment issues. I lost it. The cutting continued and the alcohol abuse. I felt it was the curse again. Things were good in the beginning, but a month into our marriage I found messages to another woman and then it spiraled out of control. There was no trust. He mentally abused me and it took a toll on my mental health. The divorce was final on February 8th, 2013. On February 13th, 2013 I attempted suicide by taking a handful of prescription pills. Fortunately, I survived. I was hospitalized for the first time in my life. I was broken, depressed and 'alone'.

I don't remember much about my stay but I do remember the good moments. For example, I felt I had no one, but it was just the lies the illness was telling me. I had my aunt. She drove me there and picked me up and then took me to Cracker Barrel where I picked up a notepad that said, "If you want rainbows, you've got to withstand the rain". It seemed appropriate at the time so I got it as a reminder to never go back down that road. My Mom and aunt visited me in the hospital. I realized at that moment in the hospital that I wasn't alone. I HAD people who cared about me and loved and supported me in a way that most patients in there with me never had or didn't have. I realized in that moment I was really lucky. I could have reached out for help but was ashamed. I accepted mental illness as my own and you should never take ownership.

Shortly before my stay, a man named Brian walked into my life or I walked into his rather. He was working at a local bar and I went in to drown my sorrows and self-medicate when we struck up a conversation. Long story short, this man brought me roses the day I got out of the hospital and cared for me tremendously, regardless of the illness. I could tell he cared and so I pushed him away, or tried to. I was still scared and sick and wanted no part of a relationship. The doctors at the hospital diagnosed me with Bipolar II Disorder again and sent me on my way with more pills. The same ones I used to try to commit suicide. Makes no sense. Regardless, I went on to date Brian and was pretty content. He saw how the medications were affecting me. He saw me black out. He saw me sleep my life away. He saw me cry. He heard me yell. But loved me regardless. So, he grew on me and I knew we had a future together whether I liked it or not.

I never wanted children, not even with my ex-husband. I felt like I was not strong enough mentally and emotionally to handle a tiny human. I feared the kiddo would turn out like me, hating themselves and wishing they were dead. I couldn't bear the thought. I mean, I couldn't even take care of myself! When I met Brian, however, something inside me changed. I trusted him. Fear kept me at bay for so long, but I knew I had to live my life. When my nephew was born, I caught baby fever. I needed a different kind of love. Permanent love that no one could take from me. So, on a vacation to Myrtle Beach, SC., low and behold, on October 31st, 2013, I found out I was pregnant. Naturally, that is when I stopped all medications. Again.

Like most new moms, I experienced feelings of joy and fear all at the same time. I wondered mostly if I would be a good mother. I wondered if this would finally 'cure' me of these illnesses I had been diagnosed with for years; to bring me the real happiness I was so desperately seeking. I worried if I would have post-partum depression the most because I didn't want that to affect my opportunity to become the mother I wanted to be. That's when I talked to the doctor about my history with severe depression and was told they would prescribe Zoloft for me once the baby was born. So, I waited for nine months to find the answers to my questions. I held my breath and hoped I wouldn't fall into a deep depression while pregnant and miraculously, I didn't! I had a fairly healthy pregnancy with a few minor setbacks, typical gallstones and kidney stones. Nothing major and on July 2nd, 2014, I gave birth via cesarean to a healthy, soon-to-be-spoiled-rotten, baby boy. Enter, stage left, Easton.

When I came to, my cousin who was in the room with me when Easton was delivered had to hold my arms down because I was having a panic attack on the operating table. I couldn't breath and I felt trapped and freaked out like I was out of control with what was happening to me.

The doctor then prescribed the Zoloft. I took it for a little while. And things were good. I had a new baby and had the love of my family, friends and coworkers. I thought this is it, it's over. I am finally ok. I'm well now, or so I thought.

My decision to be a parent was easy and it has been the best decision I have ever made in my life. When I held him, I knew everything was going to be ok and I felt real love. I knew then that I would devote my life to making him happy. I think as a good mother, you put such high expectations on yourself to do the right thing. I struggled with being that perfect mom in the beginning and it took a toll on me.

When Easton was about three or four, I noticed I started isolating myself from my loved ones. I wasn't socializing much with anyone except my Mom. My alcohol abuse started to increase. I refused to go back to being overmedicated or to find a new counselor. I didn't have the time or energy to put effort into my recovery. I was slowly starting to go downhill, but I refused to accept it at the time. My relationship and friendships were suffering and I was in a really dark place. I tried to mask the pain as most individuals with mental illness do. I was losing weight rapidly and crying a lot. The intrusive thoughts were loud and obnoxious. I couldn't shake them. But something was about to happen that would rock my world and send me into the deepest of darkest places.

On June 24th, 2018, I lost my mother unexpectedly to pneumonia, SARS and MRSA. I watched her lay for three weeks hooked to a ventilator and suffering. Her words and the sounds of the ventilator echo throughout my mind every day. I had to be strong for not only myself, but for my family, too. I was in a daze, alcohol and drug use ensued and my relationship was suffering as I rejected love. I was not medicated at all and hadn't been in three to four years. I walked around like it was ok, that she would get better. I felt numb because I knew it was the curse. The day she passed, my family was there with me, supporting me in the decision that would turn into the worst day of my life. I had to sign her off life support. The ink is still fresh in my mind. I tried to be strong for my family and for my mother. I was emotionless and downright delirious at the same time. It's all a blur and difficult to talk about to this day. But they say grief is a sign of love. I guess that means I will be loving her forever.

A few months after my Mom's passing, I couldn't take the pain. I had been so strong for so long, my mind and body couldn't take it anymore. I thought about Easton and how much he would miss me if I were gone. Maybe that is the only thing that saved me that day. But I was still so sick and in mental despair. On February 14th, 2019, I was hospitalized for the second time in my life. I went to a hospital in Lexington after telling my counselor what I had done. I had sat on my couch and held a gun to my chest for about 15 minutes, finger on the trigger, just waiting.

I don't know what I was thinking on that day. I was hurting so bad and memories of the past came flooding back. Then, as I was scanning the living room, I noticed Easton's toys scattered about. I thought about how much I loved him and how much he loved me. Who am I to take that love from him?! I cried more and then finally put the gun down.

I had an appointment that day to speak to my counselor. Luckily, I pleaded for help. I was devastated at the passing of my mother and from past emotions and events. I needed help and I asked. He said, "I really need you to trust me right now, but I am going to call the hospital." I simply responded, "ok"

While I was in the hospital, I met a lot of people going through the same thing I had gone through and some with different experiences, but I learned a lot during that time about myself. I was finally properly medicated and they officially diagnosed me with Borderline Personality Disorder and Major Depressive Disorder. Even though the diagnosis was confusing, for once in my life, at 38, I finally felt I was on track. I studied it. I learned ways to breath and to live in the present. I continued and still continue to speak with my counselor on a monthly basis. I credit him with saving my life, although he doesn't accept credit for it. He told me I chose to put the gun down and was strong enough at that moment to do so. Looking back, I feel ashamed. I knew I had a huge responsibility on my shoulders that I just couldn't get through and I knew that I have to be there for Easton. What kind of life would he have without his mother in the world? I knew all too well how it felt to grow up without a parent and I didn't want Easton to go through that kind of loss.

Mental illness is a selfish thing. It can take hold of your whole life and affect everyone you love. It is a liar, clouding your judgement and pulling the wool over your eyes. That is the best way I can describe it for me. So, I just didn't see clearly like most.

I now take six different medications and they all work for me, although I was hesitant to take anymore medication out of fear of being overmedicated again. It's like a fog has been lifted. I feel happy and grateful that I made the choice to reach out for help. I feel that I have the love and support of my loved ones and I feel like I am a better parent because of my decision to reach out. Easton is six and doesn't understand disability at this time. It will be a difficult road to say the least to explain my mental illness to him, but I am determined to do it when he is older. I think it is important to talk with your kids about disability. It's imperative because we are all different and go through different things. I don't know exactly why or how I became mentally ill. They say it is a chemical imbalance in your brain that causes you to become so ill. I do know one thing, though, life is better now that I am taking care of myself.

There are no real words to describe mental illness. Sometimes it is like you trying to meet the real you on a daily basis. What is negative self-talk and what is the real you talking? What is acceptable behavior or is this your personality? Something I struggle with is finding out who I really am. Who am I to Easton? How do I want him to perceive me and how much do I want to share with him about my disability? It's a struggle as a parent because you put so much pressure on yourself to be that perfect parent when in reality, you know, no one is perfect and everyone is out here just winging it. There's the imbalance. What your brain is telling you and what you really are.

A friend once told me to name the negative self-talk. Mine is Ted. Sometimes Ted is loud and obnoxious like before, but I know he is just a liar and I have to physically remind myself that those things aren't true. I second guess myself on little things, such as, am I good enough, smart enough, I shouldn't have done or said that. That's just Ted. And he doesn't define me. My mental illness doesn't define me and it doesn't define you as well.

If you're terrified of having a child because of your mental illness, weigh the pros and cons. Make sure you are strong enough to handle all the love they give you and believe that you deserve that kind of love! I sometimes struggled with the fact that his love is so big that my mind couldn't take it. I felt like I didn't deserve it. But I do and so do you! Choosing to have Easton was the best choice I could ever make. He has taught me so much and he is my angel and although I continue to struggle, I know waking up another day as his Mom is the greatest day.

* * * *

It's so hard being a Mama but it is so rewarding at the same time. He smiles at me when I wake him up every morning. He cuddles and is so sweet at times. And even though he sometimes has a temper and is extremely passionate, I know as a Mama I have to ensure he knows he is loved and that it is ok to express emotions as long as he talks them out with me. I know I will always love him and have his back regardless. Even when he gets angry and says he hates me I always respond, "I don't care. Cause I love you!!" Shew. Lord help me in his teenage years.

Chapter 9

Katie
A Community of Support

Katie lives in Tucson, Arizona, with her three sons.

Looking back now, I consider my life in two phases, pre-diagnosis and post-diagnosis. My life before my diagnosis now feels kind of crazy, hectic and chaotic to me. Growing up, I was a very emotional kid. I would make really big decisions suddenly and would have manic episodes and not realize it. I always just kind of thought I wasn't handling things as well as others. My parents were not really interested in therapy or anything like that for me.

In the period leading up to my breakdown and my diagnosis, I had three children, two of whom would be diagnosed with autism within seven months of each other. I was married to an alcoholic at the time. My life revolved around taking care of my kids. I was a stay-at-home mom and trying to fix my husband's alcoholism. I wanted to project an image like I had everything together. I guess I was kind of trying to be super Mom.

Then I had a complete breakdown and attempted suicide. That led me into an intensive outpatient program, where I was going to therapy three times a week for three hours. I started having this kind of self-awareness explosion, coming to terms with everything I had done and leading to something that might turn into a diagnosis. Then I had an even bigger breakdown. I was put into an in-patient program for a week and diagnosed with bipolar disorder. My whole life started to make sense, all of my actions from when I was younger; being promiscuous, drinking a lot, engaging in drugs, dating the wrong people, making these weird rash decisions, and having outbursts. It all kind of made sense. It wasn't that I was this broken person, it was that I had a mental illness. I was okay. I was coming to terms with that. Like I said, the first half of my life was just this chaotic time. Now I felt like I had some clarity.

It's still difficult. I live in fear that I will go back to that place where I was before that led me into an inpatient behavioral health program. I think that mental illness runs in my family undiagnosed. Now that I have that clarity about myself, it can be hard engaging with family members who I know have some sort of mental illness but aren't open to treatment for it or to an understanding of it. My life is definitely a daily struggle. It can be challenging, especially as a parent. I worry my kids might have the same struggles.

I was diagnosed at 29. I already had my three kids. My three sons are a total of 24 months apart. I had jumped into my marriage. Now I think I was manic at the time. I struggled with postpartum depression and then postpartum psychosis. It was very rough. I was married to a man who had an undiagnosed mental illness and was an alcoholic. He is what I would call a cultish Catholic. He follows a very conservative version of Catholicism, I guess you could say. I think I was kind of brainwashed into this religious cult, I will call it. We lived in a tiny town and there were only people from this church living there. The women had to wear dresses. If you weren't having babies all the time, something was wrong with you. They didn't believe in any birth control. I just kind of woke up one day after going to therapy and was like, what am I doing? What has my life become?

I couldn't just leave my husband when I was in-patient, but that was one of the goals that I set with my therapist while I was in there. My psychologist felt my husband was a big trigger. I was co-dependent and I was trying to fix him. My goal became "I need to get out of this marriage". But I had nothing. I was a stay-at-home mom. I didn't have any friends. It was just his family and people from church. I had to build a community for myself.

When I was hospitalized, my husband took care of the kids. My Mom flew into Tucson when she found out that I was in the mental health facility. She was not aware of his alcoholism. He was also a gambling addict. He gambled away our 401k. My mom had not known any of that. When I was hospitalized, my biggest fear was that he was going to drink and not be able to take care of the kids. I was lucky my Mom came.

It took me a about a year to plan to leave my husband. I didn't live near any family and I didn't have friends who could help. I had nothing. We were divorced a year after my impatient treatment. Parents can lose their parental rights because of a mental health diagnosis. Luckily, my husband and I had a very amicable divorce. If he had fought me, he would have had the upper hand in a custody fight over the kids because of my mental illness. There was no documentation of his alcoholism. Despite everything, I have to say he remains a good father to our kids.

When I had postpartum psychosis, I definitely questioned whether or not I was fit to be a parent. It was probably one of the scarier things that happened to me. I started becoming more and more manic and had the major breakdown. I questioned my ability to be a parent.

I take medication now, although it does not cure my mental illness. There are times when I can lose my patience a lot quicker. I worry a lot. I question my mental stability quite a bit which is another reason why I have a lot of people who check in with me. Sometimes I may think something and I'm fearful that maybe I'm manic, maybe it's not rational or something along those lines and that can be kind of scary. I really question my thoughts and my decision making. Is this a "normal," whatever normal is, or a typical way of thinking or is this me in a manic episode? It's tough being a parent of kids with disabilities, that's difficult in and of itself at times. Adding a mental illness on top of that can it can worry you even more.

My oldest son was diagnosed with autism in December of 2016. My middle son was diagnosed in July of 2017. We kind of had an idea with my oldest. He was displaying a number of developmental delays, but I was so focused on his issues, I completely lost sight of my middle son's delays and the milestones he was missing. He was actually more significantly impacted with autism than his older brother. I remember the day when I came to the realization of "Oh my God, how did I miss this?" I was advocating for my older son and learning everything I could and I completely missed all of the signs of my second son.

My kids are six, five and four now. When my two kids were diagnosed with autism, I became really manic about it. I got really involved in things and getting them services and all, which sounds great when you hear it, but I was staying up all night figuring things out and I would explode on people if I didn't feel like my kids were being fairly treated. It became more of an obsession than anything. I mean, I wouldn't trade it now because I'm a really big advocate and I'm actively involved at the state and national level, but it was consuming my life.

Until recently I was involved in a national family cohort for the early childhood education center. We developed action plans that were presented to each of our states. The action plan for Arizona was to develop a better tracking system for services related to early intervention and the resulting outcomes. I worked closely with the former director of the Arizona Division of Developmental Disabilities on that for about a year. I have been on Arizona's Interagency Coordinating Council (ICC) for about four years and have been the chair of the group since January of 2020. (Every state has an Interagency Coordinating Council (ICC) mandated by the Individuals with Disabilities Education Act (IDEA) Part C to advise and assist the Governor in developing a statewide system of early intervention services.)

I joined Partners in Policymaking (Partners in Policymaking® is a leadership and advocacy training program that teaches individuals with developmental disabilities and parents to become community leaders and catalysts for systems change). I started a support group and I met people who became very good friends. Not having family living near me has been a big challenge. I found my own community within the disability community as a whole. Meeting other parents of kids with disabilities was important. With them, there was no judgment. I felt I had found people who I could trust fully. I don't think I had ever really experienced that in my life. Having this community around me, I think it has definitely saved me from any sort of relapse. I've even considered not taking my medication at times and even mentioned it to a friend who talked me out of it. I ended up fine. I wouldn't be able to do what I do without the community that I've built. I learned that I could count on them for support. I now had my community, my support system.

In addition to my advocacy, I have a job. I'm also going to school to get my nursing degree. I know it sounds kind of manic and I have questioned that a few times, but I think I have a healthy balance now in my life. I'm able to separate and I'm able to recognize when I'm overdoing it and need to take a step back, whereas before I was pushing it. I lost a lot of weight. I was very skinny. I was picking my skin constantly. I would go for weeks without really sleeping until fairly recently. I was burning the candle at both ends.

I think one of the challenges a lot of people with mental illness have, including myself, even though I'm an advocate, is not letting people know about your disability because of fear that there might be bias. I think that if I were to share with certain people that I am bipolar, there would be a lot of bias from that and a lot of assumptions made. I have become pretty open about it, but it has taken time. In the beginning, I didn't want anyone to know, because I was scared that people would think I was "crazy." People tend to use the term "bipolar" in a negative way to describe people who are acting out or having swings. My first thought was people are going to think that I'm just this crazy person. Here I am a single mom and an advocate. There's a lot of fear around the bias that could potentially be there, if I were to share it with everyone. It can be a challenge. People can't see that I have a mental illness, but if they knew it could create bias. I had that fear when deciding to go into the nursing field. When I made the decision to work toward my nursing degree, I remember thinking 'Will I get hired as a nurse if they know I've been in a mental health facility for a week?'

My kids are too young for me to have a real conversation about my disability. When the time comes, it'll be something that I would be very open about, specifically because I want them to be comfortable with their own diagnosis. I feel like I should be the one to set the example. If they choose to not tell people, it's their choice, but I don't feel like they need to hide anything. Me being open and honest about my disability sets a good example for my kids growing up.

A psychiatric disability often has more shame associated with it. I have felt shameful about it. There are certain people I would never tell. I would never tell my employers. Unfortunately, I am unable to be completely transparent. Parenting with a mental illness is an important topic of conversation. We're not talking enough about parents with mental illness and what it entails to take care of them. It's difficult and scary. It's just a part of me. I didn't choose it. But I think I'm a pretty good parent.

Chapter 10

Christy
"Experiences with disability can make you a better parent"

Christy with her two children.

My father is a minister. My mother has always worked in social services and has been in state government for the last 20 years. I had a happy childhood. We were a solid family unit.

In high school, I began to have some depression and anxiety. In college, it began to affect my everyday life and became debilitating at times. That was when I was first prescribed medication. Early in my marriage, I had two miscarriages. That deepened my depression. After the birth of my first child, my daughter, my mental health worsened. I went on SSDI and didn't work for several years.

I had a second child, my son. A few years later, my first husband and I divorced. He moved out of state and saw the children less often. After the divorce and his move, my daughter began exhibiting signs of mental health issues herself. She would eventually be diagnosed with obsessive-compulsive disorder (OCD) and anxiety.

Before I had children, I wondered if my children might also struggle with depression. There does seem to be a strong hereditary component. I did not want them to have to struggle like I did. In the end, I decided that if they did have difficulties, I would be able to help them based on my life experiences. I think people should have children as long as their condition does not endanger the children. I think experiences with disability can make you a better parent. You can use those experiences to help your children grow. Being a parent is the best and most important job you can ever have.

I think the biggest hurdle my disability has been in parenting has been the inactivity and lack of motivation that can come with my depression. I have to constantly push myself to avoid that. I have to make sure I am taking care of myself so that I can take of my children. Even when I was not feeling 100%, I tried my best to get things done, to set a good example. No one ever wants their kids to have to struggle.

I managed to go back to work eventually. It is very challenging for me to hold down jobs. I get easily overwhelmed. I have to take care of myself, I have to take care of my daughter, I have to know where to put my focus. I taught kindergarten for three years and first grade for three years and then switched to teaching Special Education. I have also worked as an aide in special education. Because of my anxiety and depression, attendance can be a problem. I used to have panic attacks. The last school year I worked, I missed 28 days of work. The school system was wonderful about working with me. When I made the decision to quit working, they really wanted me to stay.

I decided to quit working in order to home school my daughter. My second husband and I made the decision to home school her last year. We felt she could do better with her anxiety if she was in a more relaxed environment. So far, she has done pretty well in adjusting to home schooling.

I have had a lot of help in parenting. I have a strong family system of support. My parents have been absolutely wonderful. My second husband has always been great. I have had other help as well. I always tried to do what I needed to do to take care of myself emotionally and physically so I could take care of my family.

I think society still expects more out of mothers than fathers. A father with a disability might get a pass on taking more time for himself, but a mother is expected to be there all of the time for her kids. I was a single mother for a time and in that circumstance, it is all left to the mother.

My daughter is 17 now and my son 15. When they were younger, I never directly addressed my disability with them. I think they gradually understood their mother's issues. They know I am on medication. They have adapted and gotten used to it. Since my daughter was diagnosed, she and I have discussed our issues.

Chapter 11

Morgan
"You do what works
for your family."

*Morgan lives in Florida with her husband (not pictured) and
their two sons, Royal and Roger*

I grew up in Vancouver, Washington, a suburb of Portland, Oregon. When I was 14, I started throwing up and limping. A Physician's Assistant I was seeing thought the limp was a track injury and that I was coming down with the flu. However, I had an interest in science and biology which led me to conclude the diagnosis was incorrect and I was either going crazy or had a brain tumor. The symptoms persisted. Several weeks later, I fell. My Mom was fed up. She took me to my pediatrician. He looked at my symptoms and asked me to walk. He saw pressure behind my eyes and ordered a CAT scan and bloodwork. On the way home, my Mom got a phone call in the car saying they wanted us to come back. We turned around and went back to the pediatrician's office. They put me in an exam room and took my Mom to the doctor's office where she was told I had a brain tumor. My Mom and the doctor then both came in the exam room to tell me. The first thought that went through my mind was, "Thank God, I'm not crazy."

I was diagnosed with a Glioblastoma Multiforme brain tumor on July 1 and had brain surgery on July 7. When the neurosurgeon opened my head, the tumor was like an octopus instead of being a mass of cells. It had little tentacles spread out everywhere. He took a biopsy, then closed my skull. His theory was if he tried to take out all these little tentacles of tumor, he might do more harm than good, ultimately paralyzing me. He told my Mom, "I opted for quality of life over quantity" and said I had 18 months to live. I was fortunate he didn't do more, because minimal damage was done.

My mother refused to accept his prognosis. My case was reviewed by a Pediatric Review Board. One of the doctors on the board felt the tumor could be treated at the associated hospital and questioned why I was being referred to Oregon Health Science University (OHSU), the main teaching hospital in the area. My Pediatrician simply insisted I would be treated at OHSU. I became part of a study comparing three different regimens of chemotherapy and radiation combinations. The computer randomly chose which one I received. I was assigned the one they ended up having the most success with. It was chemotherapy, then radiation therapy, then maintenance chemo.

I had four rounds of intensive chemotherapy followed by four months of radiation therapy and another four months of maintenance chemo, which is chemo in small doses. Once a week I'd get an injection of chemotherapy and then once a month, I'd have to take some pills. Fortunately, although it's one of the hardest cancers to get rid of, Glioblastoma Multiforme tumors seldom metastasize. After my initial four rounds of chemotherapy, my tumor was gone, and I have been cancer-free ever since. Unfortunately, all that treatment gave me a Traumatic Brain Injury (TBI). I have significant issues with memory and organization. In addition to my cognitive issues, I have weakness on my left side and problems with my balance. I walk with a limp and I am permanently bald.

After I started my regimen, I became part of another study on the effects of chemotherapy on the brain. They were doing cognitive tests on children prior to starting any form of treatment, testing them again at the end of treatment, then comparing the results. It was a standard operating procedure for all children to get this test at the end of their treatment, even if they didn't have the pre-test or, like in my case, got it in the middle of treatment. The exit exam became the benchmark for my cognitive impairment.

After treatment, I finished high school, went to college for an associate degree, got married, moved to Kentucky, had my first son, moved to Florida, and had my second son. I never gave it a second thought about having kids. If I couldn't have my own kids, I planned to adopt. Adoption still appeals to me. I had my boys by C-section. My first son, Royal, was underdeveloped in the uterus so they decided to take him three weeks early. He only weighed four pounds and spent three weeks in NICU. They took my second son, Roger, three weeks early, too, but that was because my water had ruptured. They both ended up being fine.

*   *   *   *

Physically, my limp is an issue in parenting. My kids walked early because I couldn't carry them. I didn't feel safe carrying them. I didn't want to trip and fall with an infant in my arms, so they had to learn to walk quickly. I didn't push them, but once they were able to walk, they walked everywhere. If it took us five minutes to get from the parking spot to the front of the store or to a shopping cart, that was the way it was going to have to be. They were going to have to walk.

I carried Roger, my youngest, more than Royal. I wore him using a wrap which made me feel more comfortable. Wraps weren't as readily available when Royal was a baby, or at least not in Kentucky. But in Florida in 2017, the trend was wearing your child with either a wrap or a sling. With Royal being so active, I carried Roger. The wrap allowed both of my hands to be free so I could catch myself if I fell.

With my limp, I can't run after my kids. I do a lot of out loud counting to ten and a lot of yelling. I hold their hands to make sure they don't get away. They know Mommy can't run after them, or at least Royal does. Roger's not quite there yet as a three-year-old. He is starting to realize it though.

My poor memory has been a larger challenge in parenting. I will tell my kids something and then forget I told them. It got worse during the COVID pandemic. Everything ran together. My memory was shot all day long. Royal is seven now. When I tell him no he can't do this or that, he will say, 'But Mom, you told me I could." My husband has been home a lot lately because of the pandemic. He'll hear me say one thing and then contradict myself the next day. He'll side with boys.

I lose track of time so I use timers and alarms to remind me of things – even daily tasks like picking Royal up from school. My memory is very visual. If I see something in one place, or I see words on a page, I can't transfer that thing to another place or those words into another book because I won't remember where it is. I will remember the first place. I use a lot of calendars and lists. I don't remember it if it isn't written down somewhere and a timer set. My phone's calendar app is the thing I use most. It's shared between my husband and I and has settings for reminders and notes.

Being a parent with a disability isn't difficult, you just have to figure out what works for you and your family. I talk to my children a lot about my disability. After all, I'm a Mom and I'm bald. Moms aren't supposed to be bald. I've addressed it with countless kids throughout my life. I'm used to it. I've just figured out how to tell my story: 'I got sick, but now I'm better and this is what I look like and this is how I function.' I have to tell kids without scaring them. I don't want them to think the next time they get a cold, they're going to end up bald and limping.

Royal asks a lot of questions. One time he asked me in the car, "Mom, why did you get a brain tumor?" I told him, "We don't know, I just got it." He continued asking if 'so-and-so' knew why, naming my doctors, parents and specific relatives, even the president. Royal's friends and classmates ask questions. I'm honest with them because there's no reason not to be. It's not something I had control over. I have to put it in perspective for them and in language they can understand. "I got a tumor, like a golf ball, in my head, and doctors tried to take it out and they couldn't. Then I had to take special medications that got rid of the tumor, but the medications hurt my brain and killed my hair. That's why I don't have any."

As parents with a disability, we have a unique advantage over other parents because we have experienced things they haven't. For example, when it was determined Royal was not thriving and I would be induced at 37 weeks, I was calm and collected. When we determined Royal wasn't tolerating my minor contractions well (I didn't even know I was having them) and we would have to deliver via caesarian section, I was calm and collected. When my epidural was administered, I was able to explain what I needed to do to get into the best position for administration. When I had to travel from my room down the hall to the NICU to see my son only an hour or so after undergoing major abdominal surgery, I wanted to walk the first time, but they wouldn't let me. The second time, they made me walk behind my wheelchair. Later my husband told me the nurses expressed to him how astonished they were at how calm I was throughout the whole process; how good I was with Royal and all his challenges related to his low-birth-weight status given I was a first-time Mom. When he told them my medical history, they immediately understood. As disabled parents, we are given the opportunity to experience a world few live in and be prepared for situations few understand.

Something I've done is bring my husband to some of my doctor's appointments and allow him to ask anything he wanted. I did this when we were first married and it afforded him the opportunity to ask his own questions – some of which my family and I had never thought of, having experienced my medical journey from the beginning. I plan on giving my sons the same opportunity if they choose.

Royal has mentioned I make Roger and him do a lot of things; like let the dog in and out or bring me something. Part of that is my parenting style – my kids are not going to sit around and have everything done for them – part is because of my mobility issues.

Hillsborough County, where I now live in Florida, has a program called Parents as Teachers where a counselor works with you and your child in your home. The purpose of the program is to identify if a child has special needs early on and assist parents in the next steps when there is a diagnosis. I signed up for it when we first moved to Florida as a 'second opinion' check to supplement Royal's scheduled Pediatric appointments. I didn't want any cognitive issues due to his birth situation to go unnoticed. Fortunately, nothing arose, and I was grateful for the monthly visits. While in the hospital when Roger was born, I was approached by the same agency and asked if I wanted to sign Roger up, which I did. It's been a great thing for them both. The counselor visits our home. They do ability checks and a learning project once a month.

Once Roger was in the system, the counselor who was coming for Royal added Roger to her caseload as a double appointment. The counselor also allowed me to have conversations with an individual trained to deal with cognitive and health-related issues as to how to best parent with a disability even though that was not necessarily the program's focus. If I had an issue with something, we would discuss it and decide on a plan. It's been a great resource, especially for Royal, but it only follows the child until they start Kindergarten. I wish there was something similar that adults could sign up for that wasn't based on a child's age, or a service to help disabled adults as parents because it really is nice to be able to have an intelligent conversation with and get advice from someone who has experience with individuals with disabilities and an early childhood education background.

Because Roger was a newborn when I signed him up for Parents as Teachers, I was required to fill out a questionnaire about myself in addition to the standard family questionnaire with Royal (asking common living situations like does he live in a house/apartment, are his parents married/divorced, does he go to daycare, and other things of that nature). According to my responses to the questionnaire, I had Postpartum Depression and another counselor started coming for in-home sessions. She had previous experience working with individuals with brain injuries and was very knowledgeable about cases like mine. She confirmed my Postpartum Depression, which I honestly think I had with Royal, but went undiagnosed. We determined that I've always had at least some underlying depression. I kind of figured that out on my own, but it was never to a point where I needed to be diagnosed or medicated. I would only have a mild flare up every once in a while. She suggested I try medication to help with both the depression and cognitive issues, so I met with a Neurophysiologist and was further diagnosed with an Executive Function Disorder, which is the diagnosis for my memory and organizational issues. None of my previous cognitive tests resulted in a diagnosis, just a list of symptoms. I was put on an antidepressant and tried Aderol then Ritalin, but I didn't like the side effects of either.

As a disabled parent I've never really received criticism. I have too much fun with my kids to allow people to notice my disabilities – at least that's what I like to think. I engage and support my kids when and where I can because I won't always be able to. When it happens that I can't, I sympathize with my child. "I would love to be able to run and ride bikes with you, but that's just not possible." I find other things I CAN do with them, like gardening, being Den Leader for Royal's Cub Scout den, and building LEGOs. My mobility issues have afforded my sons the ability to outrun me at an early age without me able to run after them. So I yell. Sometimes I can't get up or move fast enough for my kids, so I yell. My boys are rambunctious and loud, so I yell. The yelling isn't in anger, it's out of necessity: "I'm coming!" "Way to go!" "That's far enough!" We are a loud family, and it works for us. I also include my sons in my assistive technology and anything special to my disability, like my shaving what little hair I have on my head. I try to make it a fun and engaging activity they can be a part of. My sons have fun shaving my head.

There's a strong possibility Royal has Attention Deficit Disorder (ADD). My husband was diagnosed with ADD in middle school and has a family history of it, so it could be hereditary – and a HUGE challenge for someone like me. Impatience is an issue in my house – either due to my inability to move quickly, my forgetfulness, or a lack of focus/hyper focus due to ADD in others. It's stressful at times and arguments ensue, but at the end of the day, we all love each other and that's the most important thing.

I've realized something unfortunate over the years as a parent with a disability and having friends who are parents with disabilities – and even some without. When a parent isn't able to do something, their children tend to mature faster to step up and fill the gap. This happens in families who immigrate to countries that don't speak their native language. I remember my grandmother telling stories of how she and her siblings would have to explain things and translate for her parents because they didn't understand how it worked in America. I had a Deaf teacher in school and her hearing daughter learned to speak Spanish from their neighbor before she learned to speak English. Royal and Roger are having to do mature faster, too. When Royal learned how to video call his grandparents, we set up a policy that if something happened to me and I couldn't call for help, he would call his grandparents, who would then be able to call Emergency Services and together they could get help. If we had a landline, it wouldn't be as big of an issue, we'd just teach him to dial 9-1-1 like we all did in the pre-smart phone days, but with everything being digital, personalized and triple protected, he, being three-years-old, couldn't just pick up my phone and call. Again, you do what works for your family

Chapter 12

Lindsay
My story with my family and TASP

Lindsay with her oldest daughter, Juli

I was born in Indianapolis, but I have lived in Cincinnati for 35 years. I have two daughters, Julianna (Juli), who is 19, and Sara, who is 10. Sara has autism and is non-verbal. I have a partner who is Sara's father. We have been together for 12 years. Juli's father and I split up when she was young. It was a rough relationship. It wasn't the relationship that I thought that any kid I had should be around. Juli's father died from cancer about six years ago. Juli is one of my best friends. I talk to her every day.

My Mom and Dad divorced when I was very young, like three-and-a-half. I knew that my kids needed a father figure because I didn't have one when I was growing up. I have my other half now, but I didn't always choose the best relationships for me. I wanted a male figure, or a stepdad, or something. I knew that both of my girls needed a father figure. Their Dad has been a really good father figure for them.

I met my partner on-line. He was living in Florida. He came to Cincinnati to visit me. He didn't know I had a disability. I have Asperger's Syndrome (according to the Oxford Dictionary, Asperger's Syndrome is a developmental disorder related to autism and characterized by higher than average intellectual ability coupled with impaired social skills and restrictive, repetitive patterns of interest and activities). I didn't tell him anything about it. I had paid support staff, somebody at my house making sure I was organized for the day, making sure that my family had good meals, things like that. He was confused about who this person was, so I told him then about my disability and he understood it completely.

He had family living about four hours from me at the time. I fell in love with his family. He went back to Florida and told his Mom that he was going to come back and be with me. We've been together ever since. The four of us have our struggles, like everyone, but we get along together pretty well.

Juliana is working full time since she graduated from high school. She decided that she didn't want to go back to school after she graduated during the pandemic so she went to work. If she wants to go to college in the future, she can.

My family was totally against me having kids. When I first became pregnant, they wanted me to have an abortion. They thought I wasn't ready. I took some classes with a local agency and had a fake baby before I had my daughter. Let me back up. In Ohio, if you have a developmental disability and tell the people in the hospital about it, a lot of the times the babies get taken away. So, I felt I needed to be prepared to be a mother. I had a fake baby for two days, just to make sure that I was ready to have a kid. You had to change the baby, you had to feed the baby, you had to wake up in the middle of the night, and I did really well. My family was still against it, but I went on and had my baby. I have to say, after the baby came, my mother was very supportive and has helped me a lot. It's kind of funny because now my stepdad and my teenager, my 19-year-old, get along great. They have a really good relationship. I'm glad that I made the decision to keep her despite my family saying that I couldn't do it. I proved that I could.

When my oldest daughter was a child, I participated in Partners in Policymaking in downtown Cincinnati, Partners in Policymaking® is a leadership and advocacy training program that teaches individuals with developmental disabilities and parents to become community leaders and catalysts for systems change. As part of the program, we had to pick a project or issue we wanted to focus on. About that time, the case of Marcus Fiesel was in the news in the Cincinnati area. Marcus was a three-year-old with autism who had been placed in foster care. The foster agency that placed him was maybe 10 feet from where I lived at the time. His foster parents left him alone for a weekend, tied and bound and locked in a closet while they went to a family reunion. He died while they were gone and when they found him, they burned his body in a chimney and tried to dispose of his remains.

Authorities believed the cause of death was extreme heat as temperatures may have reached 105 to 110 degrees in the closet. The foster mother was convicted at trial of two counts of child endangerment and one count of involuntary manslaughter and received a sentence of 54 years to life. In his closing arguments, the assistant prosecutor told the jury the boy's life was obviously worth less to her than a dog's because they took the family dog to the reunion. The foster father accepted a plea deal and received 16 years to life. A third adult, a female, was also involved. Because she testified against the foster mother, she was given immunity from prosecution for her testimony.

The authorities started the search for him on my birthday. His story really connected with me in many ways. I wouldn't want something like that happening to any child. I want everyone to have a family and the things that go with it. Responsible parenting was the issue I wanted to advocate for.

So, the person at Partners in Policymaking hooked me up with TASP (The Association of Successful Parenting). It went under another name at the time, but it is TASP now. TASP works to support families of parents with cognitive difficulties. I quickly became heavily involved with the group, receiving extensive training on how to advocate. I went to three days of meetings in Washington, DC. They approached me afterward and asked if I wanted to be on the Board. I was like, okay, and that's how I got involved. I got to talk to people and I felt really, really comfortable. I've been involved for about 12 years now. Since I met my partner, I've done a lot with TASP. I can see how much we have built the organization. Before COVID, I traveled some with TASP. I've been to Colorado twice. I've been to Connecticut. I've been to Washington DC twice. I went to Seattle two years ago. We have an international conference every two years. Next year, it's probably going to be virtual.

My involvement with TASP has helped me grow. I was like one

of my friends. She was a woman that was always in the back of the room. She was a cocoon. Then she spread her wings. She became a butterfly. She gives talks all over the place. She goes on mission trips and things like that. She inspired me to be a butterfly for people that have disabilities who have kids with disabilities. Never did I think that something like this would happen to me.

Sara, my younger daughter, was born 12 weeks early. The hardest thing with my younger daughter is communication because she doesn't talk. I don't know what she needs unless she cries or she takes my hand or something like that. It's a big hurdle for us. I have always had good communication with my older daughter. I do things with my younger daughter, but it's a lot harder because I don't know exactly what she wants or needs all the time.

We had some genetic testing done with my younger daughter because of my disability. We wanted to get her tested. We found out her disability comes from her Dad's side. Her Dad has a brother with a disability kind of like mine. My little girl has a chromosome deletion that manifests itself as autism.

Recently, we had a situation at the Children's Hospital. Sara goes there for a lot of things. My daughter was laughed at and made fun of by a staff person once because of her disability. I called the Human Resources Department and they took care of it. I didn't want my daughter to be seeing that person anymore. I wanted somebody different.

When my older daughter's Dad died, the two of us went through lots of counseling together. I've lost people in my life, but not a Mom or Dad. The counseling has helped us bond together closer. This year, I helped provide tips for parents with disabilities on dealing with teenagers in the TASP newsletter. Honestly, my biggest tip is to just spend time with them. There will be occasions that they don't want to spend time with you, but my daughter and I have both learned through the death of her Dad that spending time together is good. And remember to tell them you love them, even though they might hate you at times. Remember to tell them that you love them, because you never know what's going to happen.

The psychologist and the parent mentor at my daughter's school have helped me a lot. My teenager went to the same school district, but I didn't know any of these people when she was young. I went to the school psychologist because we knew that Sara had a disability. The school psychologist and I have connected majorly in different ways and the same with the parent mentor. We have a parent mentor in the school district that goes around and just makes sure that the students with disabilities are getting the services they need. She and I are best friends. I have her phone number and I can talk to her about anything. She's been a big help to me.

My Mom has helped me a great deal, too. She was a single mom until I was in the sixth grade. She's helped me more with my teenager because she doesn't know how to help me with Sara because of her disability. If I have needed my Mom to back me up on anything, she's been there for me. My Mom was there when my both of my kids were born. And she's been there ever since, but she just doesn't understand how to work with Sara. I'm teaching her everyday about Sara so they can bond together. There are times that Mom and I don't see eye to eye on the parenting part, but we have learned to work together.

I have had some paid support staff from the time I became a mother. We just moved recently from Hamilton County to Butler County which has put a pause in those supports, but we are working on getting them back. (Editor's note: The following is summarized from the website of the Ohio Department of Developmental Disabilities. "In Ohio, the state's county boards of developmental disabilities provide assessments, service planning, and coordination to adults and children with developmental disabilities, as well as oversight and assistance to service providers. Services can include Homemaker/Personal Care (HPC). Direct service providers help people with household chores and personal care, including things like making food, managing money to pay household bills, cleaning and doing laundry, among other things.")

When my first child was born, I had someone coming about five hours a week. She provided some support to make my daily activities go more smoothly. We worked on budgeting and things like that because I didn't know how to keep a budget. We worked on menus. Basically, the staff helped me with budget and menus and keeping me organized, not really with childcare.

One of my support staff has been especially helpful. She hasn't worked for me for a while, but we stay in touch. She was with us for eight years, but she got a different job and couldn't work with us anymore. She called me yesterday and we had a long conversation, catching up from the last time that we had talked to each other. She has been such an important lady in my life. She brought me into a more faith-based approach about things. She was a pastor at one time. When she was with us, she lost her sister and her Dad and a few people in her life. She made me learn more about faith and keeping faith with my daughters. She was a pastor at a large African-American church in Cincinnati. She would bring us to the services and things like that.

She helped me with the childcare part because she gave me tips from when her kids were young. She gave me words of advice and things like that, things to think about when working with Sara.

I think a person with a disability who wants to be a parent should make sure they have a good partner. Honestly, you never know, there are really good men out there. And they're really good women out there, too. But you don't know to you get to know them well. That's one of the biggest pieces of advice I have to offer. I didn't have a partner necessarily for the first few years of Juli's life. That was more difficult.

People should be involved with advocacy and with legislation. If you have a daughter or a son with a disability, there are so many things going on with the political campaigns, and not just Presidential campaigns, that matter for your kids.

My teenager is aware of my disability. I have explained it to her. I have taught her that everybody's the same and to not treat a person with a disability any differently than a person without a disability. People that have disabilities should get treated equally.

We all have good days and we all have bad days. Just be thankful you have your kids because you never know. The other thing I would say is, if you can't have kids naturally, adopt. We were in the NICU for 12 weeks with our little girl. We ran across a baby that was put in foster care. There are kids with disabilities all over that need love. They need adopting.

The other thing I live by is: "Think before you speak." You need to think about it before you say it, absolutely. This is the best advice for my kids, or for anyone else for that matter!

Editor's note: The website for TASP is https://achancetoparent.net/. Lindsay wants everyone to know she can be contacted through the organization.

Lindsay's youngest daughter, Sara

Chapter 13

Ivanova
"I love my children.
They are so beautiful."

*Ivanova with her husband, Ian, and their daughters Alexandra
and Hildegard at Hildegard's baptism.*

I was born in 1988 in Soviet-occuppied Latvia. I was immediately separated from my birth mother and placed in an institution, an orphanage. I lived there until 1994, when I was five-and-a-half yeears old. We were not fed much at the orphanage. The only thing I remember eating is vegetable soup. When I was adopted in 1994, I was the size of a three-year-old. I was non-verbal, I could only babble. Nobody could understand what I was saying. An American couple adopted me. They took me back to Tacoma, Washington, and that was where I was raised in a Christian home. They raised me to know Christ.

I have autism and some intellectual limitations. I am a rocker – I rock pretty much constantly. I also have sensory issues and anxiety. When I am under stress, I have difficulty controlling my emotions. I also have difficulty dealing with the emotions of other people. I have clubfeet. I have had multiple surgeries and now have arthritis in both of my feet, which can be very painful. My orphanage records indicated that my birth mother drank excessively during my pregnancy and that may be the root cause of some of my disabilities.

It took me time to learn English. I had to repeat kindergarten twice and I was given an Individual Education Plan (IEP). My adoptive mother was the person who taught me to read in the fourth grade.

My parents were very loving, but they had a hard time understanding my disability. I had a hard time understanding my disability. There were times where it was really challenging, but one thing that was very helpful for me was that my parents believed that I could grow up. They believed that I could do adult things like get married and have children and they didn't shy away from telling me about puberty and the birds and the bees, you know, that kind of thing. They gave me very helpful information and helped me stay safe. I saved myself for marriage. I was able to get married and my parents were very supportive. I married a Christian man. His name is Ian. We met while we were in junior high school, but we didn't go to the same school. We met at church. He was very accepting of my disability. He does not have any disabilities himself. We dated ten years before we got married.

We married in 2014. We did not plan on having children, but God had a different idea. On Valentine's Day in 2017, we didn't use a condom. I got pregnant. I was scared to death. I called my Mom and she told me she would be there for me and would help me. She was very excited. There was no turning back for me. We were on this journey now. When I went to the doctor's office, the nurse wanted to give me abortion pills.

I was terrified. Since I have trouble dealing with emotions, I wasn't sure I could love a child. With my sensory issues, I thought that I would not understand my children's emotions and things like that. After I delivered a baby girl, they laid her on me. Her eyes were so big. My nurturing instincts kicked in immediately. It was the most wonderful moment of my life.

We named our daughter Alexandra. Our second daughter, Hildegard, was born just six weeks ago in February of 2021. I love my children. They are so beautiful.

I had this fear my child would be taken away by Child Protective Services right after I gave birth. I had heard from many of my self-advocate friends how that happened to a lot of mothers who have intellectual and developmental disabilities. My friends that were older had children taken from them in the delivery room. I was shocked when I heard that. I didn't want to deal with that.

When the time came for me to go to the hospital to have my babies, I made sure I had my parents and my husband and his parents at the hospital during my labor and delivery. With my support network there, they would not be able to take my child away. I always suggest to people with intellectual and developmental disabilities who are getting ready to be parents: when you're in labor and delivery, have your family there. Have people who support you there.

I have been fortunate to have a lot of support, both during my pregnancy and in helping to raise my children. When I became pregnant, I went through a Person-centered Planning process facilitated by an organization called PAVE (Partnership Advocacy Voices Empowered) to help me establish goals for myself and decide how I wanted to raise my daughter. (Editor's note: according to Carolyn Wheeler at the Human Development Institute at the University of Kentucky, Person-Centered Planning is a process which involves learning about a person's preferences and interests for a desired life and the supports, both paid and unpaid, which will be needed to achieve it. It is directed by the person and supported by others selected by the person.) That process was very good for me. I have had a lot of natural supports like my husband, my parents, my sister, my husband's parents, aunts, uncles, other family members and friends. I got better housing when my daughter was born. I received parenting classes from the Pregnancy Resource Center.

Early Head Start has been a huge help. They provided me with a weekly in-home visitor who helped me, among other things, identify my Alexandra's developmental milestones so I could see she was on track and doing well. The person taught me activities I could do with her. I have trouble realizing when my daughter was outgrowing her clothes. The in-home visitor helps me with that, too. She has helped me every step of the way. I still get weekly visits, although during COVID, the visits have had to be on-line. Now that I have had my second child, I will be entitled to weekly visits for three more years.

My local community health clinic has also been very helpful. All of the doctors there have been very supportive of me being a parent. The maternity nurse has always been very positive and has assisted me in many ways. I think I have been very fortunate to have such supportive medical care because that is not always the case.

Not everyone has been so supportive. I felt the nurses at the hospital when I had Alexandra were very condescending to me. She was three weeks pre-mature (my second child came one week before her due date). Because she was pre-mature, the nurses were fooling with her all the time. She had trouble nursing in the beginning. She couldn't suckle. I thought she wasn't getting enough sleep because they were waking her up so much and she was too tired to suckle and I told them that. The nurses threatened to keep her, to not let her go home. I learned to keep my mouth shut.

I have heard a lot of people say I shouldn't be a parent. Some tell me directly, some even yell at me in the street. Complete strangers. I remember one time at the bus stop when I missed the bus. I got upset and started talking to myself. Alexandra was with me in a stroller. An older lady started yelling at me, telling me I was a danger to my child and she was going to take my child away. I told her to leave me alone. I was trying to talk to my child, but she kept talking to me. I began walking away from the bus stop and she followed me. She kept yelling at me and threatening to call the police. It was very scary. I had to call my husband to come get me.

I remember one time on the bus itself. I take the bus a lot because my disability prevents me from driving. This particular time I was having trouble getting my daughter and the things I had with me onto the bus. People on the bus started making fun of me and telling me I shouldn't have kids. Even the bus driver was making fun of me. It was very hurtful and I started crying. I was lucky there were some people who were kind enough to help me get on the bus.

I have had hurdles in parenting, of course. Because of my sensory issues, I had difficulty with changing diapers. It was something I had to get used to. Babies wasting food bothers me. I have trauma related to food. It upsets me to see children playing with it. It goes back to my time in the orphanage when we were severely underfed.

I have a hard time controlling my emotions. I can get really overwhelmed, especially with disciplining my daughter. I know I can do a better job. I have trouble trying to chase after Alexandra. She likes to see me chase after her and pick her up and stuff, but it's getting harder for my body to do that and keep up with her because of my clubfeet.

Because of my processing problems, I have trouble understanding Alexandra when she speaks. It is getting easier as she gets older. Head Start helps me with a lot of these things.

I have flashbacks that interfere sometimes. They are linked to the past trauma in my life. Of being at the orphanage. Of being bullied at a job I had in 2011. Once, I had a friend who became homeless so I let him stay with me. Soon he was taking advantage of me and saying things that weren't true. I couldn't get him to leave. He even assaulted me. I had to get a restraining order. I still worry about degrading myself like that. I struggle with keeping the flashbacks at bay.

I plan to be very open with my children about my disability. Alexandra is still too young to understand a whole lot, but she knows many people with disabilities. I am involved in advocacy. It is very important to me. I have taken her to meetings and conferences. She has been with me often when I have been with my friends who use wheelchairs. For some time now, the meetings have happened on Zoom so she has many Zoom friends. I want her to see disability as a normal, acceptable part of life and not something that is "less than." I think she is growing up to see it that way. I worry that my girls might try to take advantage of my disability as they get older, but I plan to always be honest and open with them and inclusive.

My husband is an elder at the Lutheran Church we attend. Both of our daughters have been baptized. My faith is very important to me. I will raise my children in a Christian household, just like I was raised.

I am a parent self-advocate. It keeps me busy. I have made speeches and presentations. I am on the national Board of Directors of The Association for Successful Parenting (TASP). I have participated in a radioland podcast on eugenics. When asked by the host at the end of the podcast what I wanted people to know about individuals with intellectual and developmental disabilities having children, I told her, "I would tell them to presume confidence. To presume we could be good parents. Give us that chance."

Chapter 14

Sharon
My Life as a Single Mom

Sharon (standing, second from left) and her family.

Hello, my name is Sharon. I hail from Aurora, Illinois where I was born and raised. I'm the oldest of four children. I grew up hard of hearing. My sister was hearing, but my two brothers had hearing losses as well. We never considered ourselves as deaf because we spoke at home. Later we lived next door to my cousin who was a single mom with three deaf boys and a girl. All three boys were profoundly deaf and went to the Illinois School for the Deaf. I went to regular public schools

I'm from a family tree with Deaf and Hard of Hearing caused by genetic issues. I can trace it back to at least my Great-Grandma on my mother's side. This would have been back in the early 1900's and it continues today in 2021. Over time, I've learned that the females in my family carry the deafness gene. Growing up in my household, we spoke; we did not use sign language. My Mom was hard of hearing and my stepdad and my sister were hearing. So mostly in the house we spoke English.

Growing up living next door to my cousins who went to the school for the deaf, I was curious why they spoke with sign language and didn't understand my speech. I had to take speech classes growing up. I did not know I had a hearing loss until about the 3rd grade. Once it was diagnosed, I had to change school districts. I lived on the East side of Aurora; they did not have "Special Classes for the Hearing Impaired," so I had to attend the west side schools for the program that met my needs. With Special Classes for the Hearing Impaired, we had a teacher who knew sign language and would communicate with us. That made me want to learn more sign language so I could communicate with my cousins when they got home from school. Looking back, there were two teachers who had a huge impact on my life. They taught me my deafness should not stop me from accomplishing my dreams and goals.

I remember being so excited to communicate in sign language with my cousins. Also, I remember teaching them how to say certain words that I learned from "Speech Class." So, growing up playing with my cousins I learned to use BASL (Black American Sign Language) to communicate with them. I thank and owe my learning to my cousins.

At the age of 12 I was diagnosed with scoliosis. It was hard growing up and not being able to do the normal things. I wanted to ride a bike. I remember my Dad buying me my first bike. I was so excited I had a brand new bike. However, as soon as I got it, I was unable to ride it. I had back surgery for scoliosis and was in a body cast for 6 months at the peak of my teenage years. I'm forever thankful for Shriners Hospital in Chicago for the miracle. I was told I could become paralyzed from the waist down. But God had other plans for me. Because of scoliosis, I was unable to participate in Physical Education classes or any activities like cheerleading, basketball, track or such. Somehow, I learned to manage around the barriers I faced.

As a person with a disability and as a parent, it was hard. I had my first child when I was in high school. At the age of 16, I became a mother of a son. I hadn't planned to be a parent; it just happened and I dealt with it. At 16, you should be enjoying life with friends, planning your senior year, making college plans, etc., but that wasn't going to be me. My life was motherhood at an early age. Life changed drastically for me at that moment. I would have to learn to know when my baby was crying and I had to learn to be independent and responsible. Lucky for me, my Mom and my grandmother were my biggest supporters. They were very upset, of course, but I had to learn the hard way, like they had at a young age. I had my second child at age 20 and my third and last one at 24. By that time, I was living on my own and things were very hard.

Life was not easy being a mother with a disability. I was determined to take full responsibility for motherhood to the best of my ability. I sought assistance and guidance from my Mom and grandmother to get through the difficult times. I sought resources to help me. In the early 90's, things got a little better because technology made things a little easier. There was now closed captioning on the television (where you could buy the box to add the captions) and TTY's became available (to make your own calls without asking a hearing person and having to provide private information). Baby alert systems and all sorts of resources became available.

There are no regrets for having had a different life at an early age. I look back and remember that my mother and grandmother were with me for all three of my children being born. They are not here today. It may just be fate that things in my life happened the way they did. Growing up in Illinois and being around lots of my family helped me to understand the deaf culture and who I am as a person who cannot hear.

In 1998, my mom passed away, I was only 29, going on 30. My whole life changed. It was scarier than ever. I never thought I would be without my parents (my Dad had passed away when I was 14). Life became hard, because I was deaf and because I already had a bad back and being a single deaf mother. My Mom was always there for me to help me through the problems. Now, she was gone and I had to learn to do it on my own.

I faced barriers because I was black and disabled (deaf and scoliosis). People sometimes couldn't understand me because they said I had an accent as if I was from another country. Many times, people would ask if I was from Jamaica. Those barriers did not stop me from accomplishing what I wanted in life. I learned to use tools and resources as part of survival. Being a black person added to the struggle. Truthfully, it may not seem so, but I lived to experience these awful struggles.

In 2000, I relocated my family from Aurora, Illinois to Frankfort, Kentucky, where I remained for the next 18 years. While in Kentucky, I learned so much about my leadership abilities and my independence as a deaf person. There are NO LIMITS to what we can do. There are programs, resources, tools, and mentors to help guide us through this process we call "LIFE". I am happy that I was able to find the resources and tools to help me through this journey. In the same sense, I've given back to my community and paid it forward several times over.

In Kentucky, my leadership abilities grew and my barriers were slowly removed one by one. Being in a position to make a difference in the lives of other deaf or disabled people meant a lot to me. It also meant that by me making changes and paving a way, others would have opportunities when presented to them.

One of my proudest accomplishments was spearheading the effort to get high school diplomas for black students who were enrolled at the Kentucky School for the Deaf in the mid-20th century, but did not receive recognition for graduating. A special graduation ceremony was held at the school on August 3rd, 2011. At the time, I was the president of the Kentucky Association for the Deaf. I received a Kentucky Governor's Ambassador Award for my efforts arranging the graduation ceremony.

My children understood and loved me as their Mom. They have helped me out throughout this journey. They understood that their Mom was deaf. When you have children and your children are hearing and you are deaf, they cannot help but look out for you. My children are very understanding. My oldest two are hearing and my youngest is hard of hearing. My children have been around many members of our family and understand the difference of our disabilities. My oldest daughter would tell her friends who came to the house: "My Mom is deaf and please do not disrespect her because she cannot hear." One time my son told me, "Mom, you're the hardest working Mom. You do more work than my hearing friends' parents put together, always volunteering or helping someone." My youngest would say, "Mom I want to be like you!"

Each of my children are in a field to assist and help someone with or without a disability. My son is a barber and has his own shop. My oldest daughter will soon graduate and become a Registered Nurse (RN). My youngest is always working as a caregiver.

Today in 2021, we have so much technology, cell phones, Videophones, Facetime, Marco Pollo, Snap Shot etc.; so many different ways to communicate and remove barriers. However, since 2020 when COVID-19 hit, it has created another barrier for our Deaf Population. Face masks came out in 2020 as a way to protect ourselves from the COVID-19 disease that's killing so many people. That created another barrier where we cannot understand because the mouth is being covered. They have developed clear masks where the deaf can see and read lips and at least understand some. For me, when I go to the store or need to communicate while wearing a mask, I pull out my phone, open up Notes and type my message that I want to say. It works great for me. It will say "Hello, I'm deaf and can't hear you. It doesn't matter if you speak, I still can't hear you. I need to make a doctor appointment." That's the best way to do it for me. If there's another barrier that surfaces in the future, we will once again find a solution.

My advice to the disabled parent is seek resources and

guidance, find mentors and organizations that can support you in your purpose. Always know there are options and resources available for you.

Chapter 15
Rick and Marissa
Father and Daughter

Rick and Marissa

Rick: I was born in 1950 in Richmond, Indiana. I was supposed to be born in January, but I came in November. I weighed four pounds, two ounces. I was diagnosed with Retinopathy of Prematurity. However, there may have been a Retinitis Pigmentosa overlay. I had two uncles who died in childhood, as well as a cousin who was blind from birth from unknown causes. In college, I developed a hearing loss that worsened over the years. I now wear a cochlear implant processor in one ear and a hearing aid in the other.

Carol, who is sighted, and I got married in 1978. She very much wanted to have children. I did not think I did. It was not that I did not want them as much as I feared the responsibility. I had had little experience around babies and toddlers, and I wondered if I would do the wrong thing.

Carol had endometriosis and fibroid tumors. We tried infertility treatment and gave up when it became increasingly expensive and frustrating. We had one miscarriage in 1982.

The adoption scene looked bleak. The state list was years long, and Special Needs mostly had older children and family groups. One adoption agency representative had doubts that we would be good candidates. However, miracles do happen. On June 26, 1985, exactly two years after the miscarriage, a Wednesday's Child program featured a baby named Marissa. (Editor's Note: Wednesday's Child was once a regular feature of the local news in Louisville that encouraged people to adopt children with disabilities. It was hosted by a news anchor named Liz Everman.) She was presented as being legally blind with no vision in one eye. She was ten months old. We both said, this is our child. I called Special Needs Adoption, and they told me about the required classes, which we took. They also told us that they could give us no assurance that we would get Marissa.

We passed the home study. In December, we were considering a private adoption, but still felt that Marissa was our child. I called Special Needs and explained our dilemma. They told me that they could make a quick decision. Later that day, they called me and said, "If you want her, she's yours." This was on a Monday; we saw her for the first time that evening. On Thursday, we brought her home. Marissa was 16 months old.

One of my favorite stories of the early days happened when Marissa and I attended a Fathers and Toddlers program at the Jewish Community Center. We were asked to draw outlines of our children. I started to draw around her. She squirmed until she knew what I was doing. Then she lay quite still. An article in the paper featured a story about this experience. The beauty is that it mentioned nothing about my blindness.

Much of the way Marissa and I bonded was through reading. It started with those short toddler picture books and the books gradually became more advanced. We stopped reading together right before

Marissa started sixth grade. However, when Carol had a cerebral hemorrhage and spent two months in the hospital, Marissa asked for me to start again. I either read hardcopy braille books I got from a school that no longer needed them or I read from a paperless braille device.

One night, I was gone from home, getting my second Seeing Eye dog. Carol read to Marissa. She was not happy. She asked, "Why do you read with the light on? Daddy doesn't."

One of the difficulties of blindness was a fear that I would not know where Marissa was and she would get into something she shouldn't. One time, I was putting Marissa to bed. Suddenly, she was gone! I called Carol who was at a church meeting. She told me to keep trying to find Marissa and call her if I was still unsuccessful. I was about to call back when I heard a little voice say, "I'm under the bed."

My role in Marissa's life increased when she got older. I would help her with school projects. When she was in college, I would look at some of her papers and make suggestions. We would talk over decisions she was making, as well as triumphs and disappointments.

Being a parent who is blind leads to some awkward moments. Once Marissa and I decided to walk to a Chinese buffet that was in the neighborhood. Since she functions in the high low vision range, she helped me get my food. After doing that, Marissa became very downcast. She said, "Everyone feels sorry for me." Others saw me as a blind person and felt sorry for Marissa having to help me.

Marissa is now 36 now. We still have a good relationship. Because of my hearing loss, she has gotten interested in the fields of deafness and deafblindness. When I became president of the Kentucky Association of the Deafblind, I appointed her as secretary. When she attended Eastern Kentucky University, her original plan was to become a sign language interpreter. Because of her limited vision, she determined that this goal was not feasible. However, she minored in deaf studies. She spent a year working as an Americorps volunteer, working with people who are deaf.

Marissa: I was born in Louisville Kentucky. I was supposed to be born around November, but something happened and I appeared on August 12, 1984. The rest of those specifics, if there are any, are locked away in a file somewhere. What I do know is that a nurse named me, I was diagnosed with Retinopathy of Prematurity. I weighed one pound, eight ounces. Thanks to reconnecting with my foster sister in the last 15 years, I now have a picture of how tiny that really is.

I was a Wednesday's Child. I often think to myself that I'd like to meet Liz Everman again for a (third?) follow up and this time I'd remember her because I'm older. I'd like to thank her and show her where I've been because, let me tell you, I've had a great life so far. I don't remember being on television more than once, but my favorite aunt and uncle have played me the videotape a bunch. I don't remember being in the newspapers, but I've read them all. I don't know why the adoption stereotype still remains, but adoption in general holds a special place in my heart and it's a positive thing. I don't remember feeling different or that my family was different from any other family for a really long time.

I had not a clue that my Dad was blind and my Mom was sighted in the beginning. I just knew we always had dogs in the house and Mom did stuff that Dad didn't do. She drove a car and Dad walked with his dog. She'd cook; he'd do the dishes. She'd get the groceries; he'd clean the house. Clearly my Mom never had an issue with blindness. My parents were high school sweethearts and the blindness didn't stop her from dating him. Or marrying him after some years apart. She even jokes that she married him because he had a microwave. She wasn't burdened by reading the mail to him or having to educate people about blindness.

She was extremely resourceful and got me into the Visually-Impaired Preschool (VIPS) program when I was in preschool. She worked at the American Printing House for the Blind (APH) for several years in the educational research department. I'd like to think she did all that not only out of love, but because the world needed to understand that blindness was not a death sentence, for kids or adults.

Some of my favorite memories were those times Mom was super creative (she reads that as poor) and threw buffet style pizza parties for birthdays. Or those times where Dad beat me at cards for game night. We were always doing something fun. At some point, I caught on that Dad couldn't see and that his dog was a working dog that I couldn't play with at certain times. That was OK to me; it was just the thing to do, I guess. I think we were in an airport or a big convention center one time and I just remember grabbing his pinky because it was the only thing my tiny little hand could hold and said, "help Daddy." I was a Daddy's girl ever since.

I don't remember how I learned I couldn't see well. I was always at doctors' offices for whatever reason and I hated wearing glasses because they hurt my ears. By age three, I took them off at every opportunity I could. My parents went through so many pairs of glasses because I just kept throwing them. And then I would hide them. I do remember being at church one day when I was five maybe and I don't know what I saw or what happened, but everything I looked at was outlined in blue and yellow. Everything. It's weird because I still remember what it looked like and can draw a picture of it today, but when it happened, I panicked, screaming and crying and not knowing how to tell them what was wrong. Come to think of it, I don't know what we did about it. I mean, I was rushed to the doctor, I know, but as far as what it meant I think that's just part of being visually impaired.

I didn't have a problem with being visually impaired or with my Dad's blindness until everyone started saying "sorry" so much; like my Dad was helpless or defenseless or incapable. I took such pride in guiding my Dad places or handing him things or helping figure something out. It was always very sad and confusing when people would tell me they're sorry; sorry I couldn't see something just right or like I was burdened with always having to help my Dad out. I think the more people said sorry, the more I didn't want to know them. I felt (and still do) that there's absolutely nothing to be sorry for! My Dad is fully capable of being successful and independent and I saw nothing wrong with him being blind.

I played tricks on him, I think just to see what I could get away with like any normal kid, but he was slick about it. He caught me red-handed scaling the edge of my crib after I had told him I couldn't get out of it. I'd sneak around as quiet as I could, but he always found out what I was doing. Even as a teenager when I'd sneak back in the house well after midnight, he knew about it.

I always had a blast spending every Friday night at my parents' friends' open house. It was a fun shindig with a house full of adults and lots of them were blind, too, but it never struck me as odd being the only kid there. I didn't mind spending time around totally blind people because it always felt like the thing to do; these were funny, fun, successful individuals. They watched TV, they'd listen to or played music, they'd talk about their jobs, they'd tell jokes, and they turned their lights on for other people like me. It wasn't weird at all to me.

Sure, I had friends my own age, but I kept my circle extremely small. At some point, kids kept making fun of me for having cumbersome large print books and looking funny. They called me "retard" all the time so naturally I didn't care to be around too many people. Being around blind and visually impaired people, they got it. We didn't have to prove anything to anyone; we didn't have to fight to be just like every other kid, it was just the thing to do. We saw each other's likes and potential instead. You have a cane? Cool! I have this huge dome magnifier. You have a talking computer? Well my screen is huge font.

My vision has actually changed from when I was younger and not in the way most might think. In some ways, my vision has gotten better instead of worse. But with that, came a whole set of new challenges and struggles that I've never had to deal with before. All my life I've had to wear glasses constantly. I've had to use zoom text no matter what computer I used. I couldn't read far away or read normal printed books. I had a cane for night travel because I literally couldn't see anything at night although I didn't use the cane as consistently as I should have. Same thing with dimly lit restaurants or movie theaters; I just couldn't see where I was going. Magnifiers, monocular, bioptic glasses, large print papers, CCTV, all of that was a must every day. Something that's just considered "standard" for being visually impaired.

In 2017, I had cataract surgery on my good eye, the left one. I don't wear glasses everyday now, just reading glasses although it's still a prescription. I can read smaller size font without a magnifier, but my eyes get sore and tired very quickly. I still use a magnifier for some things especially if I don't have my reading glasses. I don't need zoom text on my personal computer at home but prefer it on any other computer I use. I can see things from farther away now but it's still blurry, and I can't always read street signs or house numbers that well. I am still night blind, but I don't use my cane. I still have some glare that throws me off if I'm not careful what I'm looking at. And the more lights I have on, the better I see, but too much light gives me a problem. And oddly enough, if I have a migraine, I prefer to invert the colors on screens to a black background instead of a white one. It's easier on the eyes.

I lost my Social Security benefits due to the vision change. I went to court to prove that I'm still visually impaired, I won, and they overturned the judge. This means that while I'm visually impaired, I no longer meet the federal definition as such; I'm just a few degrees shy. It's insane, complicated, and asinine that I went all my life fighting to keep up with my peers as a person with a disability to now fighting to prove that I still need accommodations and modifications in my adult life. It's almost like an identity crisis. I'm very lucky I have a job that I do like and I'm good at and they have done wonderfully with the little accommodations I still need, but if I were to go to a different company, they wouldn't have to provide any modifications now. I don't think I'm eligible for vocational rehabilitation services anymore. I don't even think I qualify for any disability specific grants or loans now. I'm still totally blind in my right eye and I still have a partially detached retina in my left and yet that leaves me in a bigger grey area of resources in life. I went from a strict visually impaired criteria to "extremely high partial" visual impairment.

There are different degrees of visual impairment just like there are different degrees of hearing loss. There are different teaching styles in schools because not every student learns the exact same way. I think, if anything, growing up around blindness, being exposed to plenty of people who are blind and visually impaired has made me a stronger ally and advocate for all disabilities.

Rick, Carol and Marissa

Chapter 16
Sandra
"Yes, I Would Do It Again"

Sandra lives in Louisville

My father was born totally blind. The cause of his blindness was congenital, although the disorder had not yet been given a name. Today it is known as Peter's Anomaly. He was educated at the School for the Blind in Illinois and was immediately employed after graduation. My mother was also born totally blind and it was, in truth, due to racism. Her mother, my grandmother, was having trouble when she went into labor and my grandfather took her to a hospital in Bowling Green, Kentucky. He was told she could not be admitted and he would just have to deal with it. She was turned away. My grandfather found a midwife to help deliver my mother. The midwife squeezed my mother's head too hard and damaged a nerve. That's how she became blind. This happened in 1941.

I was born in 1964 in a small town in Southern Illinois. Even then, my mother was not supposed to be admitted into the hospital, but she was let in only because she was blind. People of color were not legally allowed into the hospital. The administration didn't want anyone to know she had been admitted. To this day, my birth certificate says that I'm white.

My two sisters and I are all now totally blind as the result of the dominant genetic condition passed on to us by our father. Peter's Anomaly is rare. It is a combination of congenital cataracts, glaucoma and corneal scarring. It is related to aniridia, a condition where a person is born without irises. The difference in Peter's Anomaly is you do have irises.

My sisters and I were born with varying degrees of vision loss. The degree of loss is dependent upon how bad your glaucoma is in utero. Your eyeballs can literally burst during pregnancy. Mine did not and I was born with hazel eyes. I saw pretty well, 20 over 100, by the time I was first measured when I was ready to go to school. My sister next to me, she saw some. She could see colors, shapes and big letters. When she was about three, she started having very bad headaches and she would say, "Don't tell Mommy." She was scared. I didn't say anything. I now know the headaches were due to glaucoma. She became totally blind. I will always feel guilty about not telling my mother about the headaches. When my next sister came along, I was 13 years old. I watched her like a hawk and anytime I noticed anything, I would tell my parents that something was wrong with her. Some of her vision was saved. Nowadays, she can see better than I can.

Hearing issues are also connected to Peter's Anomaly and my sisters and I all have some degree of hearing loss.

I was 16 when the glaucoma really started for me. I was attending the Kentucky School for the Blind. I was telling people at the school I couldn't see anything, everything was white. The school personnel initially thought I might have a psychiatric issue and I was evaluated for that. I was told it was in my head. My headaches by this time were so bad that I would often physically become sick. I was finally taken to an eye doctor who told me I had glaucoma. My eye pressure, which is supposed to be around 12 or 14, was measured at a minus 65. The pressure was very painful. I was put on medication. I don't know how long that medication had been in use. It is now known that one of possible side effect of this particular medication in women is infertility. No one told me. I had no idea. I took massive doses of this to ease the pain and keep my vision. After I was married and was trying to have a baby, they didn't know why I couldn't conceive. They went through the lists of medicines I had taken over my lifetime to that time. I was 22 or 23. They concluded that it was that medicine that had caused my infertility. My inability to have a baby was one of the reasons my first husband left me.

I always wanted to have children. When I was five, I used to say I wanted five kids. I wanted to have two and adopt three. I always wanted to be married, have a big family and give kids a chance. I think I was 16 when I first saw Liz Everman (a Louisville television news anchor) on Wednesday's Child, a regular feature of the local news that encouraged people to adopt children with disabilities. I remember watching it in the living room and saying, "One of these days, I'm going to do that."

After my divorce, I ended up trying the marriage thing again, even though it didn't go so well the first time. After I remarried, my second husband and I went through the Kentucky State adoption program to become certified as foster parents with the hope of eventually adopting. I was very excited. We were in a decent financial position. We had a nice house and everything. I was working at an independent living center and he was a blind vendor at an IRS building. I had a room all planned. We didn't have too much trouble going through the program. We were both visually impaired, but we had decent vision. No one really said anything to us about our ability to foster or adopt.

When we finished the classes, they were going to place a little boy in our home. I believe he was two. I was probably 30 about this time now. I was very excited even though the child wasn't going to come from my own body. I had made a Crayola crayon room and wrote stories for this kid all during that time. I told my husband that a child was ready to be placed with us. He told me he was going bowling and never came back.

Since his income was more than mine, I was in no position to take on a child. Needless to say, I had to turn down the placement. I lost my house. I had nothing. I told the folks with the state that when I got my life back together, I still wanted to foster and adopt. I would just do it by myself. I don't think they believed me.

In 1999, the state started a new program. If a child was placed with you, you would get first choice to adopt to prevent the child from moving from home to home. I decided to try it. I'd already done most of the classes. I just needed a few new ones. I think I finished with the classes in February of 2000. At the end of that month, I got a call saying, "We have a blind baby, and he probably has other issues. Do you want him?" My sight had gotten somewhat worse. I assumed they were trying to just give the blind woman the blind baby because nobody else wanted him. I said yes.

Most people have nine months to prepare for a new baby. I had 36 hours. I had nothing for him because they had told us in the classes we could probably expect a tiny, newborn baby. The only thing I had was a bassinet. They brought this baby straight from the court with a half-full sack, which didn't have anything of much use in it. I was frantically calling friends to see if they had anything I could borrow.

He couldn't sit up. He couldn't crawl. He was pretty much limp. He could reach but it really didn't seem to be intentional. I had just started a new job with Louisville city government. I had only been there for about six weeks and I was already asking for two weeks off. The Mayor at the time, Dave Armstrong, was very good to his staff. I was allowed the time off so I could arrange services for my new son including neurological tests and that type of thing. I was bound and determined I was going to be the best parent I could be for however long I had him.

I grew up with blind parents, so I never thought there was anything I couldn't do. I had friends who could help me. When I first got my son in my home, my co-workers invited me to dinner and bought me a big gift. I always have had support from friends and professionals. One co-worker in particular, Lindsay, was a great help. She would drive my son and me around when we needed transportation. She was in the courtroom with me through a lot of proceedings. I was very fortunate to have very good friends.

I ended up keeping him in foster care for almost two years before his mother's rights were terminated. At that point, I adopted him. I was in and out of court a lot because members of his biological family would come forward and say they wanted him. I remember one appearance before a judge specifically. This aunt and uncle had come forward saying they wanted him. We're sitting in the courtroom. In the middle of the proceedings, a bailiff brings in an officer. The officer said, "Your Honor, we have some evidence that needs to be brought to light in this proceeding." The judge said, "Okay, you may proceed." The night before the hearing the uncle had been caught soliciting a male prostitute. The aunt, his wife, had no idea and started screaming and hitting him in the face. They had to be taken out.

I remember another proceeding. The biological mother of my son had psychiatric and intellectual disabilities. At one point, her mother was trying to get custody of her grandson. When the issue of drugs came up, the grandmother got up and yelled, "We never exposed that baby to drugs, we always did our drugs in the basement." The judge at that point said, "We are leaving the boy in the custody of Miss Williams. He's thriving." The mother turns around, leaps over the chairs, grabs me and screams "You've got my baby!" It was like a Lifetime movie.

My son always scored low on IQ tests. In my opinion, the tests are biased against a whole lot of people. I was with him recently when he had one. The tester said I couldn't say anything which I agreed to. I sat there and listened. They asked him what the word tranquil meant. Who uses the word tranquil? How many people know what that word means? When we got home he asked me what the 'T' word meant. He knew it started with a T. I told him what it meant and he said he missed that one. The tester asked him what was the same about a boat and a car? I don't know what the right answer is. I think it's something about their both modes of transportation or something like that. I thought his was a better answer. He said they both have motors. Why is that wrong? It's not.

He is now 21. I went through all sorts of physical things with him because of his various disabilities. I was even told by one doctor, after I'd had the tests on him to see why he was the way he was, "Oh, he's just a foster baby. You can give him back. Nobody will judge you if you give him back. He'll never know you. He will never be able to walk or talk or be anything." Wow. He can walk and talk and he definitely knows who I am. He has intellectual challenges, but he is capable. He is trying to do what he needs to do to become employed. He does way more than anyone ever thought he would and he can be very insightful.

Although he was eligible for another year of school, I pulled him out last year. He was around too many of the wrong influences in school. These kids can have some psychiatric issues at his age. He was a very good athlete, a Special Olympian who even set a record. But he hurt himself, and kind of lost his identity. He's been lost for a while. He actually did a whole bunch of things that no one ever thought he would have the mental capacity to do, not that they were good things. He left for a time, basically living on the streets. He has been back with me now since June. We're getting his vocational rehabilitation case reopened. He's back. He's doing well. He's taking his medications.

About three years after I got him, I started fostering a girl child. When you foster or adopt children, you are able to tell them what children you are willing to take. Do you want one who's blind or deaf? A child that uses a wheelchair? A feeding tube? I really couldn't accept a child with physical disabilities because I had stairs. I thought that would be harder for me to deal with having my vision impairment. I also didn't want someone who had been sexually abused.

Contrary to my wishes, the girl that came to me was a product of a very abusive environment and a child of trauma. As it turned out, she could be very violent. She was very, very gifted in some ways, very artistic. She could sing, draw and paint. That creative and artistic side of her was developed even as a three-year-old. She could even sew as a three-year-old. But she had very significant issues. At age five, she was put out of public schools. Because of her trauma and her violent acting out, people would tell me, this is the worst case we've ever seen. I maxed my insurance out at a million dollars when she was ten. I went through a whole lot of legal stuff to get her the help she needed and to keep my son safe because she would try to harm him. I had to make really hard decisions as a parent. Which child do I keep? Who do I sacrifice? Am I sacrificing the son if I try to keep the daughter? They're six months apart and it was like raising twins.

I made a very difficult decision when she was ten. Because of the insurance, I could no longer afford even for me to get sick or hurt. She needed help desperately. I agreed to put her in the care of the state. I was told it would be a good thing and she would get the help she needed. It was better for me financially, but I told them, if I do this, I want to keep my parental rights. I was her mother, no matter what problems she had, and I would not let them take my rights away. The state agreed. I remained very involved with every aspect of her life. She would hurt people when she would stay in the facilities where she lived. She hospitalized many people. She put one lady in intensive care. It was almost like watching a person possessed. It was horrible.

My daughter now has two children. She has a very severe psychiatric disability. It's sad to say, but I almost wish the children could be taken from her so that she could get the help she needs. It's just so sad because no child needs to grow up in the situation those two are in.

She has one child and the father has the other. She ran away at 15 from where she was at the time and started living on the streets. She met someone, he was 27, and got pregnant when she was 16. She came back home to me right before she was to have the baby. Pregnancy and a psychiatric disability are not a good combination. I let her stay with me until her baby was born. She tore my house apart. She ripped the doors off and the windows out. That was about two-and-a-half years ago. She went to the hospital to have the baby. I was with her. She had several meltdowns in the hospital. After she had the baby, the hospital did a psychological evaluation on her. She was railing and ranting at me. They deemed her not to be a danger to herself, but they were unsure about the baby. They wanted the baby in a safe place while the girl got some help. I said I would take the baby. We went before the judge, but the judge ruled that I was incompetent because of my blindness. I was only wanting temporary custody. I didn't want full custody. I just wanted my daughter to get the help she needed and get in a program where she could get assistance in taking care of the baby. The judge gave my granddaughter to the father, an alleged drug dealer.

While this was going on, my daughter did me physical harm. I ended up in the hospital and actually went into hiding for a time. I had not heard from her in a couple of years when she called saying she needed my help. She had given birth to her second child by the same man, although she didn't put his name on the birth certificate. She had custody of her second daughter, but she had gotten into trouble. I took the baby for six months.

When I got my granddaughter six months ago, I had nothing for her. I did not know that I would need to go retrieve a baby. I called a friend of mine because she has a big, burly military husband. I did not want to be around my daughter alone. I can't be. I asked if they could go with me to pick up my granddaughter. Their response was "We'll be there in an hour." I called friends with children or grandchildren to see what I could borrow. This happened to be at the outbreak of the COVID-19 pandemic. I had all these people dropping stuff at my door so I would have what I needed to take care of her. My friends are my support network.

My granddaughter left a couple of weeks ago. When she first came, she seemed terrified. She was about nine months old. She was afraid of being left by herself. I got her to trust me. By the time she left, she would look at me and laugh and shriek and talk to me in her baby talk.

I was always a single mom. I chose not to date anybody for 18 years. I didn't want anyone to have to deal with my kids and I didn't want just anyone around my children. I was very particular who they were around. I did my best for them and to help them grow into adults. I often think about whether if I had the opportunity to do it over again, would I? I'd have to say yes. As challenged as my children are, especially my daughter, they might have spent their lives in institutions. They would have never gotten to have an example of what a family was or what it was like to get a hug or go see Santa or ride on the ghost train at the zoo. They got to do all that stuff because I did all that stuff with them. So, yeah, I would do it again.

* * * *

Jumping forward nine months after the initial interview, much has happened in my life with my children and grandchildren. During this time, I have had the opportunity to be a part of my eldest granddaughter's life. She stayed with me for three months. Having two little girls under the age of three was both exhilarating and exasperating at the same time. Having little vision made it challenging.

My oldest granddaughter appeared to be dealing with some of the same issues brought about by trauma as my daughter had dealt with at that age. She screamed for hours when I brought her to my home. She would eat nothing, having only been allowed to eat only fast food. My offering her apples sent her into rages. I spent the first week with her showing her that I was the adult, and she was safe and was allowed to just be a child. She was so unapproachable and almost unlovable. I spent many nights alone in my room with the girls asleep in the other, crying since I felt so unattached to this little person whom I felt hated the ground I tread upon.

After some weeks, this little person began to follow me around. She would reach out and touch my hair or my hand. One night, I remember her coming to the rocking chair where I was rocking her little sister. She touched my knee. She looked at me and said, "I sit on your lap?" Tears filled my eyes and my heart as I lifted this very-big-for-her-age little girl onto my lap. She tucked her head beneath my chin and nestled close. They both slept.

The children are gone now. My daughter had one of her episodes, for lack of a better word. She accused me of allowing her children to be abused while in my home. No rhyme. No reason. It just was. I found myself being investigated by the Kentucky Child Protective Services. Of course, the allegations were found to have absolutely no validity.

I last saw the girls the day before Thanksgiving. Christmas was quite sad. I had already purchased and wrapped gifts. I know nothing about my daughter or her two little girls since then. I do know that my daughter is expecting another baby girl at the beginning of April. Same father of the baby so I am fairly certain that the scenario will be the same. My heart hurts for all of them.

Chapter 17

Carrissa
"It never crossed my mind that I would not be a parent."

Carrissa with her four-year-old son, Will, and her husband, Ben.

I had a wonderful but crazy family life growing up in Fancy Farm, Kentucky, and I always wanted to experience that as a parent. I learned very young that there is always a path to getting what you want.

My family tree is kind of... well, let's say it has a lot of branches. I grew up with my mother and my older brother in Fancy Farm. My Dad left when I was two years old, so for a while, it was just my Mom, my brother, and me. When I turned 10, my mother met my current stepdad who I call my father. He had three kids of his own. I went from a household of three to a household of seven. My biological father had several other marriages later. I have two other half siblings, one a sister that I haven't seen since she was two years old.

My biological father was adopted and I think that influenced my decision to adopt. His adoption was closed and he did not learn about it until he was much older. While that may have been a good choice for his family, I wanted to do things the exact opposite way. I now have an open relationship with my son's birth mother. Kentucky does not recognize open adoption, but we have an agreement with her for her to see him once a year and she does keep up with us in other ways. I want Will to know through my family and through her that families are never conventional. I want him to know how much love went into his coming to be from all sides. Maybe I'm getting a little ahead of the story.

My transition to a larger family was quick. I had a tenth birthday slumber party. I invited the girl who would become my stepsister. My brother was friends with her brother and her sister was my babysitter. All three of them ended up over at our house that night. The next thing you know, my mother said to their father, "You might as well come over, too, since your kids are all here." He asked her out that night and one month later to the day they were married. So, that was really quick. It was a little difficult at first, meshing ourselves together. Now we don't consider ourselves stepsiblings. We are just siblings. My sister and I are six months apart and we were raised almost like twins for the rest of our childhood. It was a little chaotic in a two-bedroom trailer. The older sister went off to the army not too long after my mother and stepfather were married.

I always wanted to be a parent. That was always on my radar. It never crossed my mind that I would not be. I was always the girl that played with the baby dolls, always played house. I never thought anything different. So, I just assumed, like anybody else, that once I got married, I would have kids, no ifs, ands or buts about it.

It's funny how I was raised. My mother impressed upon me that I could do anything. I was no different than anybody else. That's just how it was. I did chores, I did whatever. I just had a disability. My grandmother, on the other hand, always had the idea that I was special. She assumed I would always stay at home and live with my "Mommy" all my life. She flipped out when I decided I wanted to move out.

It was funny how that happened. I had just graduated from high school. My mother and I were driving one day and we passed some apartments. There was a "For Rent" sign out in front and I just happened to say, "I wonder what it would be like to be out on my own." My mother did a U turn and went right back to the apartments. Two weeks later I was out.

She never gave me a minute to ever question any decision about what I wanted to do because she knew if I thought about it, I would tend to think about all the scenarios, negatives and positives, and might talk myself out of it. If I wanted to be in a dance competition, I did it. I did all these things. She would let me do them. I attribute my personality and my decision-making to her.

I married in college. During the semester of my internship when I was finishing my Bachelor's degree in Social Work, my husband and I wanted to stop contraception. I went to the same family doctor I had gone to for years. During a routine exam he asked about a refill of my birth control and I told him I didn't need one. I told him I wanted to start a family because I was getting ready to graduate. He proceeded to tell me that that would be dangerous because he had a brother with cerebral palsy (CP) and he knew how difficult the condition was. He felt like I couldn't handle having a baby. Those actual words came out of his mouth.

Needless to say, that was the last time I saw that doctor. We felt we were ready to start a family since I was about to graduate. Nothing changed about what I wanted. I found another doctor and we continued. We had been married for about a year and a half. Nothing happened. After a year, I went to see someone new. I wanted to know if the problem had something to do with my disability. The words from my previous physician still lingered. I questioned whether CP was the problem. She said it wasn't, but that I was probably too stressed about it. Two years later, still nothing. Finally, we got tested and, long story short, I was not ovulating like I should. I went on fertility treatments for over a year. I'm one of those people that hang on to a dream of any sort. Like a dog with a bone, I never give up.

During those treatments, I had to have blood work every month. The technician who did the blood work would preach to me every time about what I was doing. Maybe God (or whatever higher power people want to call it), she inferred, was telling me I should not do this because I was disabled. She said that to me every month and I left in tears every time because I felt like this was another way that I was broke, if that makes any sense. I requested, and got, another technician.

After about a year of that, I decided that I needed to take a break. We stopped for six months and started trying again. Still nothing after another year. I told my husband "Look, we have to go another route because I can't take this anymore." I was on an emotional roller coaster.

By that time, I had started working at an independent living center. I heard of a study that had come out about how parents with disabilities were having their children taken away from them at higher rates than non-disabled parents and how couples with disabilities were being discriminated against when trying to adopt. I was doing a lot of research, on other forms of fertility, on foster parenting, etc. I suggested to my husband we should try fostering.

I found an agency through Catholic Charities that did adoptions on a sliding scale. The agency would first put a couple through foster care certification, then place a child into foster care with parents of the birth families choosing for a period of time before permanently placing the child for adoption. The child was a ward of the adoption agency until the foster parents were determined to be a good fit. The agency worked with the birth families to terminate their rights. Once the agency felt you were going to be good parents, they released the child to be formally adopted.

Ben and I decided to go to what we thought was an introductory class. Little did we know that after that weekend, we were certified to become foster parents as long as we completed the home study and did a few other required things. We decided we might as well go for it. That was what influenced my decision to adopt. Long, long story short, we completely stumbled into adoption. We just wanted to find out more and then, lo and behold, we were taking steps to adopt.

I thought the hardest thing would be the adoption itself. It happened very easy, believe it or not, so much so that all my reservations were just totally unfounded. When I first talked to the social worker, I thought she would judge me, but she had worked with the father before and told us we would be fine.

As you go through this process, you make a book about your life. The agency gives it to the birth families. The family selects three possible families from the books they receive. The three families are then interviewed by the birth family and they decide with whom they want to place their child.

A family is almost never picked the first time. A lot of people have to be recertified after 10 years. But we were picked the first time our book was in circulation. We were interviewed and chosen right off the bat by the birth family. I had thought no one would want to place their kid with someone they considered broken. I thought I was going to have to prove myself just like I always had. I fully expected it to take a while. I prepared myself for all that, but none of that happened. The only pushback I got in the whole process was not from the birth mother. It was from the agency. They were a little hesitant about how I did certain things, like how I would get him in and out of his crib or how I propped him up in his bassinet so that I could pick him up. The agency dragged out the process somewhat just because they wanted more visits to make sure it was a good placement for him.

I have encountered challenges that I know my friends and other people typically have not. I feel like I have to prove myself to anybody who asks a question: how are you going to do this? A baby? How are you going to get him out of the crib? How are you going to change a diaper? It is almost like I'm always on an audition of some sort. I feel judged, though people may not mean to be judging. They may just be curious, but if I don't have the right answers or demonstrate confidence, their judgments may lead to other things. I feel like I need to have everything figured out. I had to do a lot of research into adaptive changing tables and adaptive cribs and looked for other peer role models who did things differently, not necessarily how my mother did it. It was difficult because there was not a whole lot out there. There is not a lot of research, there are not a lot of parents with disabilities groups. There is more now but when I started, there wasn't. It's sad to say, considering parents with disabilities have always been around. I have found connecting via social media to be very helpful.

Like I said, I always feel I have to prove myself. I have thought that about every aspect of my life. I react to it differently as a parent than I do for myself, simply because it affects more than me. Being a mother, I also feel like I have to be responsible for everything because that is the typical social role of a mother. There are times I get sad when there's something I cannot do or there is a limit, but Will has always adapted to those limits better than I have. To him, I'm just Mom.

When people realize that he's adopted, it is like this sort of light bulb goes off and you can almost hear them think: "That makes sense now!" Then they immediately start asking questions about his birth mother or, as they usually say, his "real mother." They start talking about how hard it must have been for her or how amazed they are that she chose us. I am not downplaying her feelings in the least. I know what she did. I don't know if I could do it. I will always love and respect her for her decision. But I will always be Mom. And for the record, my fertility issues were not disability related! So that's really irritating.

It's not that I am not used to people judging me all the time, but you get that mama bear instinct. You know when you're with your kid you just want to protect him, no matter what. People are not attacking just me at that point. So, rather than being a teacher, which is what I was always taught to be, I become raw mama bear and want to do things differently.

There have been instances that have been difficult for me. When he started head start, I wanted the Trick or Treat outing to be accessible for his Mom because I am that Mom that wants to participate in everything, sometime to my son's dismay. I got feedback from teachers about having to wait for me and I had to educate them on the Americans with Disability Act (ADA). I also had to educate a couple of daycares about having their entrances accessible. In the first case, on the first day he went, there was a big gumball machine at the door and I couldn't get my wheelchair through the entrance. The instructor joked with me saying, if somebody would come smash the glass in the door, she could get it fixed. Needless to say, he was not in that daycare long. I am not going to do business with a business owner who won't do anything about accessibility.

Another daycare was in a brand new building. Totally accessible, or so we thought. That is why we picked it. We didn't realize until after we placed him that they decided for security reasons to have a keypad. That is fine. I can use a keypad, no problem. I understood. But the keypad was not on the sidewalk. It was in a grassy area next to the door. I suggested an easy fix so I could use it. They did not think they needed to do it. Needless to say, he got pulled from that daycare right after I submitted a formal complaint demanding a plan to fix it. I had already reported it verbally. They had 90 days to come up with such a plan, but the complaint was dismissed because the court said the company had legitimate reasons for not being able to change it. I didn't believe the reasons were legitimate, but I couldn't prove it. That is why he does not go there anymore, all over a keypad you can go to Lowe's and get. I don't understand that. I need to go back and see if they ever did fix it. Those are challenges that I face. I sometimes worry that he is going to be held back because of me. I hope not, but I do have anxiety about it.

When he was a baby, I worried about a lot of things. How will I adapt to be able to pick him up? How am I going to teach him to walk as a parent that doesn't walk herself? How am I going to do a lot of things? As it turned out, he adapted to me more than I had to adapt to him and he did it so easily. He learned quickly how to pull up on Momma. If he wanted Momma, he knew how to get up. We have got pictures of him pushing a cart that had a tray in front where toys could be carried. He would turn it around and sit in the tray, pretending he was in a wheelchair.

We were already thinking about crawling from probably his second week. We were already thinking about walking when he finally learned to crawl. He could barely make two steps and we were already concerned about running off. I am not saying he was perfect. There was one time he got out the front door and ran across our busy highway and I had to chase him because I was the only parent home. There was another time that he rolled out of his adaptive crib because I could not get in front of him quick enough. He was quicker than me. He rolled out on the floor. It was my worst nightmare. How am I going to pick him up? I didn't even have time to think I just grabbed him by his shorts. That is the kind of worries that you have, but there's no time to worry about it when it actually happens. You know, Mom instinct just kicks in and you just do.

He had his first developmental test. He was behind on a few things and one of them was climbing steps. We had no steps in our home. He would always use the ramp with me wherever we went so he didn't know how to climb stairs. They had to show him. That is just how he lives.

Once, he has asked me "Are we going to ride in daddy's truck, Momma?" I had to tell him, "No, Momma can't ride in Daddy's truck." I've gotten the question once or twice: "Do you ever walk, Momma?" I just say "No, Momma can't walk." He was fine with those answers until recently. He has started asking me more questions. He recently told me that "Momma could walk if she would just try hard enough." That came from us always telling him to try. I'll try to explain to him that Momma gets around differently. He also asks from time to time if my legs will ever be fixed. My response is usually something along the lines of they don't need to be because I have my chair. Just like if one way didn't work for him doing something, we would find a different way to get it done. But there will come a day when that doesn't satisfy him.

I worry that things that are unfair for me are automatically going to rub off on him. He started soccer this year. Most of the time the fields are muddy. Mom is left on the sidewalk and he keeps running to me to let me know everything he is doing. It's nice to know he still wants to include me no matter the situation, but I do feel left out even more now when something is not accessible. I never get a break from my job!

Sometimes he will bolt from his dad. He will run off, but when he is with me, he stays right with me. He will bolt from his teachers, so much so that he is known as a runner, but he doesn't do that with me. They are all amazed. It is like he has developed some kind of intuition. I'm blessed in that way, I guess.

I have questions about when he enters elementary school. What is going to happen there when he starts to realize Momma is different? Is he going to get teased? Is he going to be ashamed? You know, I still have those insecurities. I'm trying to raise him not to be that way. But you never know, kids can be cruel.

I don't think service and government agencies think about parents with disabilities. I think it's the last scenario. I honestly think that we're just now catching up to where we should be equal. In the work world, in society, they don't think about us being parents. When you talk about parents with disabilities, people automatically assume you're talking about a parent with a child with a disability, the opposite scenario.

I don't think society has any expectations about parents with disabilities, if you want me to be quite honest. I think society is not prepared. There have been parents with disabilities for many years, obviously, but it's not the norm. You don't see it on television. It is still very novel. You don't see it out in public. Well, you may in bigger cities, I don't know, but I am from a small town. You may see a few but it's not prevalent. Oh, I got looks a lot when he was a baby. I even got comments. Once, I was in a doctor's office waiting with my son. I was singing to him just to keep him occupied. A lady, an older lady across from me, said to me, "Is that your brother?" I said, "No, it's my son." I just kept on singing and playing with him, whatever I needed to do. I heard her whisper to the woman sitting next to her "They shouldn't have allowed that to happen." That was so sad. She pointed directly at me and I knew what she was talking about. It took all that I had in me not to go 'mama bear' on her. I just stayed there and kept on singing until I was called.

Another time, I was in Walgreens. Will was still in a nice carrier. I was going around the store with him just sitting there in his carrier. When I was done shopping, I went out of the store. I put him in his car seat and got into the driver's seat because I drive from my chair. Somebody beat on my window. I didn't know the person; it was an older man. I cracked the window and I said, "Can I help you?" He just says, "I saw you carrying that kid in the store. Is he yours?" I said, "Yes." He says, "That's amazing. I just don't know how you do it." He went through a litany of how surprised he was. And then next thing I know, he asks if he can pray with me for a minute. Now I learned a long time ago, people like to pray over me. People try to pray the disability away. I have tried to argue with it or say no, but they just keep on praying. Now my response is to shut up and let them do it and they will soon go away. I closed my window and left him to sit there and pray. I guess it was so amazing to him. He had never seen it before. I think it is still kind of a sideshow thing, unfortunately. It's getting better. But I don't think we're there yet.

In addition to cerebral palsy, I also have severe anxiety and some learning disabilities. I was made fun of badly as a child. Kids would let the air out of my tires. I got books thrown at me for being different. It would make me cry and little boys thought that was funny. I saw a counselor. I developed a sense of understanding of the disability community. I am proud most days now because I have learned that it is just a part of who I am. But those insecurities are always there. I don't think they will ever completely disappear. I know I can do things. Now I know society is broken.

The ADA certainly has helped me. I could not have fought the daycares like I did without the ADA. I could probably not get into my son's school. I can remember being little before the ADA and having to switch schools twice because the schools were not accessible and they didn't have to be. I am not having to fight the battles my mother did. I mentioned earlier the study that found parents with disabilities have a higher rate of being determined not to be able to take care of a child. You know, those kind of studies scare me because I feel like no matter what I do, I am always on audition.

I think the ADA has really helped things, but we have a way to go. Bakers still think that they should not have to provide services to people because they are different. Teachers still think that they should not have to make Trick or Treat activities accessible for Mom. I should not have to educate the park that the T-ball dugout should not have a bump in the entrance, but I do. Why? Because I am there and if I am having that problem so will somebody else. I am lucky that this is also what I do for a job so it makes it a little bit easier. I can fight some of these battles on the clock, but without the legislation that is there, none of that would be possible. It is still kind of just getting everybody on board with the fact that it exists, 30 years after the ADA was signed.

My advice for people with disabilities is "Go for it!" We are all different. Support really helps. I know just talking to some of my coworkers who are parents with disabilities has helped. It's like wow, suddenly your small world just got a whole lot bigger and having that support really helped me. Right before Will was placed with us, I had a co-worker who I knew quite well and who was also a wheelchair user say to me, "You know, I have a grandson. It is really difficult for me to handle him. I don't think you can do it." That shattered me. I am proud to say she was wrong, but without other positive feedback from other people that worked with me, it might not have gone so well.

I have to talk about what I am going through now. I am on the Personal Care Attendant Program (PCAP) (Editor's note: PCAP is a Kentucky state program that provides personal care assistants). The state is requiring everyone on the program to sign up for Medicaid so PCAP can be payer of last resort. I don't qualify for Medicaid because of my income, but the state is still having me apply. Apparently, the program wants me to sign a part of my income over to the state of Kentucky so that I will qualify for Medicaid and be able to get waiver services. I don't know what will happen. I'm currently fighting it because I want to be able to keep all of my income and work full-time.

I have a fear that I could somehow lose the family support that I have, the support of my husband and my parents. Maybe some of this is irrational, but I do have anxiety about it. I feel like I will have to quit my job in order to get the services I need to provide for my child. How fair is that? I have worked hard to be able to become employed and get off the "system," get off SSI and SSDI. Then there are all these Medicaid cuts that might be coming down the line that could affect parents with disabilities. It affects anybody with a disability. You know, the legislation always is going to trickle down to the average Joe. It is really unfair, because people don't hear the personal stories enough. I am not asking for anything more than a real life. I am not asking for anything that I feel like I am not entitled to. I am just asking to be a human being and hopefully in the process, raise another human being that is going to affect and change society's way of thinking. I hope there are a 1,000 Wills being raised that will change this world. Who knows what he will have to tackle?

Chapter 18

Denise
My Daughter Grew Up in the Movement

Denise, Melissa and Pat

Pat and I met in 1972 at Brooklyn College. He was recruiting members of the disabled students' organization, S.O.F.E.D.U.P. (the Student Organization For Every Disability United for Progress) to attend a demonstration against Richard Nixon for vetoing the Rehabilitation Act. We both had disabilities. I was a polio survivor and he had spina bifida. We were wheelchair users, although I used crutches for the first 20 years of my life. Both of us were deeply involved with the disability rights movement.

We got married in 1975. We wanted to have a child and tried to get pregnant, unsuccessfully, for about five years. We never tried fertility treatments or anything like that. Nothing was happening so we just stopped trying. When we had been married for 13 years, we decided to adopt rather than try again to have a child naturally. You have to ask yourself: is it about being able to prove you can physically have a child or is it about having a family? We chose family. Actually, I think adoption is pretty natural.

We went to an adoption agency in Albany, New York, that had a minority adoption program. Pat was Puerto Rican and I am multi-racial. We were concerned how the adoption agency might view two disabled people trying to adopt. We wanted to know if that was going to be an issue. Pat approached the adoption expecting difficulty. He was prepared to be a strong advocate.

We were lucky enough to have found a social worker who had just taken over a program that had been struggling with placement of children in homes of minority families. She was inexperienced, but that was a blessing because she didn't have the prejudice and pre-conceived notions that many other folks might bring to the job. She was young and new and wanted to make this program work.

Pat came on strong in our discussions with her. He told her we would make good parents. We both come from large families and had experience taking care of our own siblings as children and infants. If there was a problem or she felt that our disability was in any way having a negative impact, he wanted to hear about it. She was probably a little intimidated by him, but we ended up having a good relationship. She said, "Well, you know, as long as you guys meet all the criteria, go through the interviews with the social workers, and make sure that the home visits and everything else are fine, I don't see a reason why you shouldn't be able to adopt a child." I think we were very lucky. I think the timing was one of those things that was on our side. She was new to the area and new to the program. I think a lot of that energy helped make the adoption happen.

Melissa was placed with us nine months later. She was three months old and had been with a foster family. As I said, it was a minority adoption program. Melissa was biracial. Her biological father was African-American. Her mother was around the same age as me at the time, 34. She wanted her child to be raised in a two-parent family and felt she couldn't raise a child as a single parent. She read our case study and our profile and chose us to be the parents. I think she felt that we had a pretty stable family environment. She knew we had disabilities.

Pat was a planner by nature and by training, so we tried to plan ahead for all the things that we would need in terms of the house, accessibility wise. We made sure we got a crib that we could pull the sides down. They weren't making accessible stuff for parents with disabilities then, but we managed to find one that we could manage to get her in and out of. We had to make sure that we always had something we could carry her in, like a snugly.

I think that you always face challenges with people's attitudes, people being surprised, first of all, that you can even have a child. We never made it a secret that we had adopted her when she was an infant. Later on, she was a little confused about it. We just let the story go, you know, until she was old enough to have it explained to her. When she started school, I think one of the things that frustrated her was that everybody always assumed she was adopted. At the time, she didn't think she was.

We had to deal with the surprise that people expressed that we could have a child or that we could raise a family. How was it possible? When she was in kindergarten, I remember the kindergarten teacher telling us our daughter was doing a lot of socializing in class. She said to me, "Well, you know, Melissa always wants to help the other children. I'm sure she gets that because she has to do that at home. Sometimes it's hard to get her to focus on her own work." I looked at her and I said, "Melissa does not take care of us. She's a kindergartener, she doesn't have to worry about taking care of us. So, if she needs to be focused, you need to tell her to just pay attention to her schoolwork. You need to work on her excessive socializing." She was assuming this behavior just had something to do with her having parents with disabilities.

This kindergarten teacher was a trip. One time, we went to attend an event that was going on with the kids, some production in the classroom or whatever. I was running late, as usual. While I was getting out of the van, she apparently made an announcement to all the families. She said, "Well, we're going to wait a couple of minutes more because Mrs. Figueroa is getting out of her van. You know, it takes a little bit longer for her." Another parent told me about it. It was infuriating. Oh my God, did she need to do that? The woman just had a hard time adjusting to us. I think she just felt uncomfortable and couldn't talk about it. At one point, I had to confront her about it. I just said, "There was no need to say anything, you could have started the program. You didn't need to wait for me and, if you wanted to delay it, you could have done so without saying why. You didn't need to point out my disability and make Melissa feel like she was something different." So, that's the kind of stuff that was very frustrating.

There was always the feeling you had to educate people about your whole life as a person with a disability. What do you do? That's why I have been the director of the Independent Living Center of the Hudson Valley (in Troy, New York) for more than 30 years, but not a lot has changed when it comes to attitudes.

Another issue as a parent of a small child was taking her to playgrounds and other public places. It was always very difficult and frustrating because nothing was accessible. Even when they tried to make the playgrounds accessible, you couldn't get close enough to the playground equipment. And when your child is very young, you need to be nearby if they fall or something. It was a challenge, trying to find a place that was accessible that Melissa would want to go to and where she could interact with other kids. She did go to daycare because Pat and I were both working. Pat was working for New York State and I was at the IL Center.

We had an accessible van so it wasn't hard for us to get in and out with her and manage the car seats. Neither of us had disabilities involving our upper body extremities. We were able to lift her and carry her and do those things without help. We didn't have personal assistance services so we didn't have the battles I know some people have had about how you can use your home care worker for assistance with your child, is it allowed or not, you know, that sort of thing.

We didn't really have much assistance. We relied on friends to some extent. We certainly had friends who helped us if I was going someplace like a playground or whatever where I wanted to be sure somebody was with me in case I couldn't manage. I didn't want to risk her safety. There were times we couldn't do things because of our disabilities because something wasn't accessible. Melissa would want to go, but we would have to tell her we couldn't take her there. She was going to have to wait until somebody else could do that. The lack of physical accessibility was the biggest issue for us.

As she was growing up and wanted to go to friend's house or something like that it was a bit of an issue. Most parents want to get to know the other parents, right, but we couldn't get into other people's homes. We'd invite people to our house sometimes for birthday parties and such for the kids, but parents couldn't reciprocate because their houses were not accessible. You don't really get to develop a relationship with them like anybody else would.

Letting her go to other kids' houses was always a worry for us because you didn't know what household you were sending your kid into. She'd want to go visit and play and it's like, well, I have to trust that these people really are okay. Both Pat and I were from New York City, where you didn't really do that sort of thing and we were somewhat concerned about unknown places. I was always worrying about that kind of stuff; that she would end up in a place where I couldn't get to her if she needed help.

I used a buddy strap to keep Melissa close when she was a

toddler and I was out with her. Pat and I both used a buddy strap. Luckily, they did that in her daycare so she was used to it. The children had to hold a rope or something like that when they went for a walk. She was used to her buddy strap so that helped a lot.

Melissa was very comfortable with operating the lift in the van from an early age because she would watch me do it so often. That made my mother nervous. My mother had mobility issues and Melissa wanted to operate the lift for her. My mother wasn't so sure about it. I told her not to worry because Melissa knew what she was doing. Melissa learned quickly how to climb up into the wheelchair to get in my lap. She liked to sit on the foot petals. That was often her seat.

One of the things Pat and I talked about before having a child was that we didn't want our child to feel like they had to take care of us ever. We really worried about that. We weren't going to be raising our own home attendant. Obviously, family members help each other out, and maybe we erred on the other side of not having her help. She couldn't clean her room for anything. For us, it was important that we make sure that we were her parents and that we were taking care of her and she didn't feel obligated to take care of us.

*   *   *   *

As I mentioned in the beginning, Pat and I were deeply involved in the disability rights movement. In fact, he was the director of the first independent living center in New York back in 1978. Melissa grew up in the movement. I served on the board of the National Council for independent Living (NCIL) for years. NCIL has an annual conference in Washington, DC. Part of the conference every year is a march to the White House. Hundreds of individuals with disabilities march to advocate for their rights. Melissa's first march was in 1989 when she was four months old. She was on my chest as we wheeled to the White House. That particular march was to support the passage of the Americans with Disabilities Act. It was pouring rain that day. I remember trying to keep her dry under a garbage bag.

She grew to love going to Washington for the marches and demonstrations. She went to every one she could while growing up unless school interfered. Once we moved it to summer, it didn't interfere. After the march one year, she went back to day care chanting, "Hey, Hey, Ho, Ho, Nursing Homes Have Got to Go!" They had to wonder what that was all about.

In 1991, I became President of the NCIL Board. I had to go to quarterly meetings. I took her to almost all of the NCIL Board meetings. My friend, Marcie, who was also involved in the movement, would travel with me. While I was in meetings, she would watch Melissa. Many times Melissa just sat on the floor during the meetings and colored or whatever.

She was around the movement quite a bit. Melissa grew up around disability. We certainly talked about disability with her. Most of our friends were in the movement and had disabilities. In our household, we talked about disability rights all of the time. She was very comfortable around disability, whether people had CP or they were blind, or they were deaf, or whatever, she was familiar with pretty much every kind of a disability. She knew our disabilities, she knew what each of us could or could not do.

*   *   *   *

In 2012, Pat went into the hospital for elbow surgery. He never came out. That was a real nightmare. He ended up becoming septic in the hospital. It was definitely disability-related. He was getting catheterized and ended up with urinary tract sepsis. He never recovered from it and we lost him too soon. We had a great life together.

Melissa got her undergraduate degree in Special Education in 2011, then got her Master's degree in ESL (teaching English as a second language), but she has really focused more on special education in her career. Since her Dad was Puerto Rican, you might think she grew up in a bi-lingual household, but he did not use much Spanish.

She is working at a non-profit in Albany, ironically, in a program called the Vocational Daily Skills (VDS) program. She works with kids with mental health disabilities, helping them to transition to adulthood. So, it's doing independent living skills, like her Mom. She's running that program and another program where they help kids who are in the community try to link up with services. It is a mental health population that she's working with and some kids with learning disabilities as well.

She is married and has a four-year-old son. Just like his Mom, he learned quickly to climb into my lap on the wheelchair and he uses the pedals as a seat. He knows not to touch the joystick of the power wheelchair I now use though. That took a little bit of training. He just spent the weekend with me. At that age, they need constant attention. As a matter of fact, at one point, I was talking to my sister-in-law, and he said, "Grandma, you have to focus on me." It is a joy to spend time with him.

I would tell people with disabilities who are thinking about being parents, "Go for it." Being a family is a wonderful experience for anybody. I think sometimes we all focus too much on ourselves. I would say, yes, you should do it, you should explore what adaptive things you're going to need, be honest with yourself about what it is you can do and what you can't do so you can plan ahead of time. I really encourage people to not be afraid, but to plan. Find out what the resources are around you and make sure you've got everything in place. I don't think that there's any reason that you shouldn't have a family. It's a lifetime commitment. Obviously, you don't have children to resolve your own issues. You need to be doing it for the right reasons. But it's a great experience, I have absolutely no regrets about it. It continues to be a blessing. I have my grandson now. Maybe there'll be others, who knows.

It continues to be a great adventure.

Pat and Melissa

Chapter 19

Kathy
Chasing Happiness: I Couldn't Ask for More

Kathy with her husband, Jim, her daughter Bri and their dog, Baxter.

I was raised in a small town in Vermont. I would spend the summers staying near the waters of Lake Champlain and the winters shivering and waiting for summer again. I grew up with the same set of friends. We all started kindergarten together and we all graduated from high school together.

When I was a toddler, I have some vague memories of walking. But actually, the memories I have were more around walking and falling. I was diagnosed with spinal muscular atrophy and, when I was five, I got my first power wheelchair. It was an Everest & Jennings, and it was shiny and fast. I knew I could get things done with that chair. So, life went on.

I was always the hub when we played 'whip' at school. One kid would hold the handlebar on my chair, holding hands with the next kid in line. Eventually, we'd have a 20-person human chain holding on for dear life as I started to slowly spin my Everest & Jennings chair, changing direction and watching and waiting until the poor child on the end would let go, sailing off at a high rate of speed. Good times.

I was highly motivated in school. I wanted to be smart. I wanted to be popular. I wanted to work with horses. It often seemed that the expectations of others about what was possible for me weren't as high as my own. It wasn't until after I graduated from high school that I found out that I had met the requirements to be a Governor's Scholar, but that my guidance counselor never told me. By that time, I was already in college. I went to the University of Vermont, graduated summa cum laude, and got accepted to Cornell's doctoral program in Equine Nutrition. But Ithica, New York, sounded cold and intense to 21-year-old me back in 1991. I was looking for some adventure.

To this day, my parents insist that I promised that I was only going to move to Lexington, Kentucky, for six months. I fell immediately in love with the Bluegrass State. It was warm, people called me "hon" (which I thought was very sweet), and horses were on a pedestal. Literally. Monuments to horses everywhere and an entire state park dedicated to all things equine.

Lexington was where I learned to drive a car. Well, it was a van, initially. Back home, I was told that the technology I needed wasn't available. My strength has never been so great, and even with reduced effort steering, I was going to be dangerous at any vehicular speed greater than the five miles an hour my chair would go. But in Lexington, I was able to drive with a joystick which gave me control over the accelerator, brake and steering. It was just like the joystick on my wheelchair, but opposite. It only takes speeding up and blowing through one stop sign when you think you are applying the brakes to figure that out. Driving gave me true freedom. I could go to work. I could go to a drive thru at McDonald's. I didn't have to wait two hours on the Wheels bus. I didn't have to justify myself – to anyone.

When I was 26, I met Jim. He was an automotive mechanic who

worked down the street from my apartment. I had brought my car in for service and we chatted a little. I told him where I lived and he let me know that he often jogged in that neighborhood. I told him to stop by to say hello the next time he was out jogging. That night, he knocked on my door. He had on shorts and running shoes. He also appeared pretty winded. We talked for a bit and then I had to drive him home. Turns out, he wasn't a really big jogging enthusiast, but he was enthusiastic about me. I've only seen him run one time since then and that was the day one of our horses got loose. The rest, as they say, is history.

Jim and I got married in 1998. I found out who my friends were and who I didn't really know as well as I thought I did. Several people were very concerned about my well-being. I had one friend with a disability ask me if I was marrying Jim because I was worried no one would ever want me. Another said that Jim was an incredibly special find, because well, you know, who would marry someone with a disability. Ouch. One friend has not spoken to me since I announced we were getting married because she assumed there was something weird going on.

So, it's good to get on firm ground and reassess relationships with the world from time to time. Having done that, we went about building our lives together. I was still pretty driven. I had gotten my Master's degree in Rehabilitation Counseling from the University of Kentucky and a job at that same university. With full-time employment came more educational opportunities. I took advantage of that and pursued and completed my Doctorate in Educational Psychology while working full-time. My desire to work with horses hadn't faded, but I had a hard time breaking into the horse industry in Kentucky back then. So, I let horses be the fuel for me outside of work. We bought some land, built a barn, and lived happily.

The ever after part was nagging at me though. I wanted a family of our own. I did a lot of reading. I went to the high-risk obstetrician. I kept reading and asking questions. What I discovered was that, while I was pretty confident that I could sustain a pregnancy, I was far less confident in what the medical providers were telling me. Their expectations for success for me were lower than mine. They were so focused on my disability that they couldn't consider the idea of someone in a wheelchair having a baby. I didn't think it was a good start when the doctors were more freaked out about the idea that I would want to become pregnant than I was. But I did also realize that I didn't have the financial means to venture out beyond my healthcare coverage to find healthcare providers who would be allies in my pursuit.

For several years through my 30's, life was about work and farm life. The days were more than full and busy. I set ongoing goals for myself and felt good about accomplishing them. I'd cross them off my list and move on. Succeed and proceed. I also felt like a did a lot of growing up in my 30's. I liked being responsible for myself and for the responsibility that went along with being part of a 'we' in marriage. I got to connect with a lot of students through work, had friends that I spent time with, and continued my journey with horses – breeding and showing on a small scale. I sought out challenges to keep me occupied.

Life was enough. Every now and then, Jim and I would talk about kids. We wondered aloud if we would want to adopt. When I made the decision not to get pregnant, I also decided not to second guess it. My nature has always been to overthink, lament and to make sure I take everything into account. When I make a list of pros and cons, I weigh all the items, because not everything should count the same, right? My fancy mechanism for decision making was one where I could always make the pros and cons come out even. I don't follow easy answers. But in this situation, I gave myself some grace. The decision about not having babies was made with the best information I had available. No regrets. Maybe wondering "what if" in the dark when it was quiet, but, ultimately, I was at peace with the decision.

However, Jim and I would always return to the conversation of growing a family. We knew we had to be on the same page at the same time. That took a while. As my career responsibilities grew, work, teaching and horses took up a lot of time. Jim had started his own business which meant he always had some activity or other filling his days. It was 2010 when we decided that adoption might be a route to take. I jumped in to looking at private adoptions as well as the state process. Given the vast needs that were present in Kentucky, we decided to become a resource family for the state.

Reunification is always the first priority for children when the state is involved. Given this, prospective families are asked if they want to be considered 'adopt only.' We opted for this. That doesn't mean any guarantees, but it does let all involved know our overall intentions. We went through the required training, along with about 40 others in our group. We made connections that we've kept to this day. The shared experience was a powerful one. The motivations of people to provide foster care seemed to vary widely. We settled on the idea that maybe a toddler up to a five or six-year-old would be in our wheelhouse. Our house wasn't set up for sibling groups and we were maybe feeling that keeping up with an infant would be tough for us.

So of course, the first call that we got was to foster an infant boy and toddler girl sibling group. Their mother had been an active drug user when the boy was born. He would wail at night, as his tiny body dealt with withdrawal. It was like when the lights went out, he would start his night job. Nothing soothed him. He was miserable. We felt helpless. They did not stay with us for long, as their biological mother was working through her plan to get them back. After they left, Jim and I took a couple of long naps, until the phone rang the next time. Over the course of the next year, we continued to foster sporadically. Then we got the call about a child who didn't fit with our plan. That's how most good things happen, though.

A state worker shared information on a teenager named Brianna who loved animals and wanted to be a veterinarian. We talked with her a couple of times and then met her and her worker for lunch. It was the official meet and greet. We fell into a relaxed conversation pretty quickly. We talked about animals and cooking, favorite places and favorite foods. By the end of that month, she moved in. It was all a bit of a whirlwind.

I would tell people that we had a new bouncing baby 13-year-old girl when we got word that we'd been approved as a resource family for Bri. We missed out on the cuteness of little itty bitty kiddos and jumped right into middle school. What a culture shock. There weren't any bottles and pacifiers, but talk of hair colors, belly button rings and tattoos.

We couldn't share pictures, couldn't provide specifics and ultimately couldn't share much information at all about the new addition to our family until we adopted her. That took two and a half years. During that time, we spent lots of time talking, sharing, and trying to help Bri set her own goals and learn how to accomplish them.

The whole system of foster care and youth who find themselves in that system is complex and difficult. As a parent, I did feel very well equipped to learn about the legal aspects of the adoption process and advocate when needed. That being said, it still took a very long time for the adoption process to happen. Bri was 16 when she was finally 'officially' our daughter, but we didn't need the document to become a family. Being a teenager is no picnic, even in households where you've grown up with the same people your whole life. Then transplant yourself into new families, with new dynamics, new game plans, and new everything, maybe for years, if you're in foster care. I'm still impressed to this day by her resilience and her strength.

There were several mental health diagnoses that brought lots of services. Some of the services were good. Some were downright appalling. I learned that quality mental health care is not available at 1:00 in the morning. I learned that I could still pull an all-nighter, when necessary. Some days, I even thought that maybe I knew what I was doing.

As a parent with a disability, the most frustrating interactions seemed to happen when we'd go for medical appointments for Bri. I always felt like the doctors and nurses were more interested in me. Usually, there was that moment of surprise when we'd get called from a waiting room when the medical assistant saw that I would accompany her. Then there was usually a moment or two when they tried to decide if I could speak and would ask Bri questions to "ask your mom." "Why don't you ask her yourself? She's sitting right there," would come the biting retort from Bri. I always found myself half proud and half cringing.

Bri is a huge animal lover. With six horses, three dogs and assorted barn cats, that meant there was always something to do, and always something to talk about at home. Evenings and weekends were spent in the barn, getting a riding lesson, or walking, cleaning or feeding somebody. We worked on providing a solid home base and opportunities to explore interests and build skills.

It has been a really interesting journey thus far. Bri graduated high school in 2018 and now is living in Cincinnati and working as a veterinary technician. She got a driver's license and a car just before she turned 21. That took a while. There are so many other options for transportation, she wasn't in a hurry. I still don't get it, but if she wasn't ready to drive before now, then it's probably best that she didn't, right? She drove home to see us a couple of weeks ago, to get food and celebrate her 21st birthday. She asked me if we plan on adopting any more kids now that she's out of the house. She says it would be kind of neat to be a mentor for a younger kid, but that she's also very happy with the way things are. I am, too. I guess time will tell. The journey has been about chasing happiness and wanting good at every turn. I couldn't ask for more.

Chapter 20

Jane
My Children Helped Me a Lot

Jane with her two daughters, Natalie and Janea

The first person I was around who had a disability was my grandmother. Granny had polio when she was in her teens and it affected her mobility. It did not affect her ability to have three sons, one of which was my Dad. Granny also had twin brothers who had developmental disabilities. One of them lived his entire life with my grandparents. The other twin lived with Granny's oldest brother. So, I have always known people with disabilities. I am thankful for that because it shaped my life. I grew up in an environment that was not biased towards disabilities.

In high school, I started working at the home office of the Dollar General Stores. I worked there ten years doing bookkeeping and payroll. Both of my daughters were born while I was an employee at Dollar General. When our youngest was born in 1985, we made the decision that I couldn't stay at Dollar General because I was working up to 20 hours a week overtime. It was not conducive to having a three-year-old and a newborn.

I was able to find a job as a secretary at a law firm in 1985. I really enjoyed that job. Ironically it led me to my lifelong career. One of the owners also owned apartments and one of them was rented to the son of a secretary for the Kentucky Office of Vocational Rehabilitation (KYOVR). She would come to the law office to drop off the rent for her son's apartment. She told me about a couple openings with the state. I got a job as an administrative secretary in the KYOVR regional office.

Soon after I started, I took advantage of an employee benefit of tuition for college. The courses had to be geared toward a career within in the agency. My career plan was to become a vocational rehabilitation counselor. With the support of my husband, Herb, and my daughters, Natalie and Janea, as cheerleaders, I finished my degree in ten long years. It took perseverance, but to be honest it took my entire family. They helped me study and they understood when I had to miss functions.

I graduated in 1997 with a Bachelor's Degree in Psychology with a minor in Business. A year earlier, I started to have some health issues. At first, I thought my extreme fatigue was just due to burning the candle at both ends, but then I started having tingling in my left hand and my left leg would go to sleep. My primary care doctor referred me to a specialist at Vanderbilt. The neurologist there ran a battery of tests over several months. I was diagnosed with Multiple Sclerosis in May of 1997, the same month I graduated from college. Our daughters were 15 and 12 at the time. My diagnosis was difficult for all of us. I was in an MS exacerbation at the time with leg pain (I describe it as a fire inside) and my vision was blurred. I was prescribed a high dose IV steroids to circumvent the symptoms. It worked and it continued to work periodically when the MS would relapse up until two years ago.

At that time, the MS became progressive. Treatments don't help as much they did for the 21 years I had relapsing, remitting MS.

However, I still have good days and thus far I have maintained my independence.

After I graduated from college, there was a vocational rehabilitation counselor opening in the KYOVR Bowling Green office. I became a counselor in August of 1997. I loved being a counselor and helping people with disabilities gain employment. I even handled the paperwork pretty well since I had been an assistant for 10 years. In 1998, I enrolled in a Masters in Rehabilitation Program at Auburn University. This was the first time I faced discrimination due to my disability. There was an employee of OVR's central office who said to me, "how will you be able to handle the stress of doing a Master's online with your disability?" I was stunned. I had "handled" being a high producing counselor with my disability so I saw no reason I couldn't do the Master's program like my colleagues were doing. That ordeal shaped my career. I knew then it was wrong and, if it came from within the agency, discrimination was bound to be other places. It gave me the fire to someday be able to affect changes. I finished my Master's program with a 3.75 GPA in 2000. I passed the Certification for Rehabilitation Counselors and worked as counselor in Bowling Green for several years.

I had several relapses with MS, but was able to work through most of them. When I did have to be off work, I was blessed with good coworkers and a loving family. During a relapse in 2010, the County Clerk in Allen County, where most of my consumers lived, offered me office space for free so I could limit my travel. My supervisor at the time helped to get me equipment as an accommodation to let me work there. Soon, the agency opened an office in the county and I was asked to supervise it.

In 2012, an opening for Director of Program Services in the KYOVR central office became available. I moved into an apartment in Frankfort and started that October. My husband kept his job as machine operator and stayed in our home in Allen County. We did a lot of weekend visits. I loved the Director job. I always had worked hard, but I think during the three-and-a-half years as Director I worked harder than ever. It was rare for me to work less than 45 to 50 hours a week. I had great staff around me and it was rewarding work, although the political side of it was not always easy. I like to think I made a difference during that time. I retired in May of 2016 when I turned 55.

My children were in their teens when I was diagnosed with MS. I think the limitations of my disability affected them because they had to help more at home than most of their friends. I just was unable to work and do everything at home, too. It also affected them when I couldn't go to events due to fatigue or pain from the MS. But I also think it helped form their strong work ethic and shaped them into the people they are today. I would not change or wish away my disability because I think it helped me be the Mom, wife, daughter, and worker I am. It gave me a perspective I would not have had otherwise.

Our oldest daughter, Natalie is an Assistant Principal at the primary center here in Allen County. It has about 1,000 students from Preschool through 3rd grade so she stays busy. Natalie and Shane have one son, Aidan who is 15. Our youngest daughter, Janea, followed in her Mom's footsteps and is an assistant at the Office of Vocational Rehabilitation in Glasgow. She loves working with the staff to help people with disabilities gain independence and employment. She has three sons Will 16, Blayne 14, and Ace age 12. She and her husband, Evan also co-own a swimming pool business in Allen County.

If I can give any advice to a person with a disability it's to be active in an organization where you have avenues to advocate. During my career, I saw advocacy in action through the passage of the Americans with Disabilities Act in 1990. It greatly improved many aspects of life for people with disabilities and I truly believe peaceful protest helped get that legislation passed. I also think the parent advocacy for children with disabilities is evident in the Workforce Innovation And Opportunities Act which reauthorized vocational rehabilitation in 2017. The law is much more focused on serving youth than ever before in vocational rehabilitation. Again, advocacy works.

Earlier I noted that my MS has progressed. It happened slowly, but in 2018, I had an exacerbation that I have never really recovered from. I have lots of fatigue, pins and needles in my legs, and vertigo probably 60 to 70% of the time. This definitely has affected my family. My grandsons are very active in sports and other activities. Unfortunately, I have had to miss most of their games. But I cheer them on from home. Since COVID stopped their sports, I have felt less guilt because I was not missing out. See, you've got to find the good in everything, even a pandemic.

Chapter 21

Jimmy
In the Blink of an Eye

Jimmy with his family in Sellersburg, Indiana

I did not acquire a disability until I was 43 years old. Before that, I was (or at least I thought I was) a relatively healthy and virile individual. On the evening of March 29, 2019, I went to sleep feeling relaxed and excited for what laid ahead in the days to come. I had just returned from a work-related conference in Washington D.C. The evening before my family and I had traveled to Plainfield, Indiana, and we were staying a few days with friends while the kids were on Spring Break.

I woke up on the morning of March 30, nauseous and vomiting. I assumed that it was just a stomach bug and that it would pass. I had just spent the days before in the airport, at a hotel, and in the Nation's capital. It never fails that the kids bring home a bug around this time of year, too, which is why we normally took our family vacations in the fall. Never in a million years would I have thought I was in the beginning stages of a full-blown massive heart attack. What transpired would forever change my life and that of my wife and two children. It has affected all of us in different ways, both physically and mentally.

I do not remember much of what happened over the next several weeks post heart attack. Everything that I do know is what was relayed to me by my wife, family, doctors and by reading my medical files. Today, I read the files or listen to the stories as if I am reading or hearing about someone else. I do not comprehend that it is about me. I think that is for the best and is probably why I have not had a complete breakdown mentally! I have the scar down my chest and the constant ticking of the mechanical heart valve to remind me.

My wife took on all the worry and made all the medical decisions for me. She was the one that had to make the 90-minute drive back home with the kids while I was still in the hospital. She was the one that had to take on the role of both parents, while continuing to work and driving back and forth from Southern Indiana to Indianapolis every chance she had until I was able to be released. She was the one that had to hear that along with the heart attack, I also had multiple strokes in the back of my head. She was the one that had to hear that IF I survived, they were not sure what my cognitive abilities would be. She was the one who had to hear that the stent was a success, but my vitals were not improving. She was the one that was told that my heart valve had ruptured and a mechanical valve was my best option. She was the one that was also told that I needed that surgery IMMEDIATELY in order to survive, but because they had already started me on blood thinners due to the stent, they could not do the surgery until they could wean me off the blood thinners, which could take three to four days. She was the one that had to wait for the medical team to decide if I would even be a viable candidate for that surgery. She was the one that had to sign off on the forms when I was placed on ECMO life support to bridge me until they could perform the surgery. Not every doctor on the medical team was in favor of the surgery and/or the ECMO, so she was also the one that had to wait for that decision. All I had to do was sleep… and keep living, of course!

In all I spent 54 days in the hospital. I was transferred to the Frazier Rehabilitation Center in Louisville for another two weeks for Occupational Therapy (OT), Physical Therapy (PT) and Speech Therapy. I then had an additional two months or so of outpatient OT, PT and Speech after I was able to return home.

I made it home just in time for my daughter's middle school band recital. She and I were both excited that I was able to get to see her performance. Her grandfather came up from Bonnieville, Kentucky, to watch it, too. I was still not able to walk long distances at that time, so a co-worker lent me a wheelchair. Having worked in the disability field since 1999, it was no surprise to me how people with disabilities were commonly treated. However, this was the first time for me to experience it firsthand. I was lucky enough to find a spot in the front where I could kind of see, but you can be certain that no one offered to move to make a spot. I had to take what I could find. Once I found a spot, several adults and children practically climbed over me to get to their spots, no one asked if I could move or said, "excuse me." However, I did get to see her perform! Unfortunately, her grandfather was not as lucky. He is a double amputee and uses a wheelchair, too. As with me, no one offered to move or give up his or her spot so he could get his wheelchair into the gym to see her performance, so he could only listen from out in the lobby.

Shortly after returning home, my son had his annual day camp for Cub Scouts at Tunnel Mill Scout Reservation in Charlestown, Indiana. I had always taken that week off in the past to volunteer as a Den Walker at the camp. It was a time for Austin and me to spend together, just us guys, doing guy stuff. I was not able to go this time around. As I mentioned above, I was still not able to walk long distances, much less spend all day out in the heat and traverse the terrain of the campground. He had to go at it alone this time. He did fine, but I know it hurt him as much as it did me that we were not able to experience that together.

Next came soccer. Austin plays in both a Spring and a Fall soccer league. His soccer games are at a sports complex in Jeffersonville, Indiana. They have about 10 fields. Austin's games were on one of the farthest fields back. I went to as many games as I could, but I was never actually able to watch. I was walking independently by that time, but was only able to walk about 200 or so steps before I had to stop. Realizing that if I made it all the way to the field, I would then have to walk that same distance back, I always ended up stopping and sitting on a bench. I could just barely see the field and could see the players, but could not really tell what was going on. Nevertheless, I was there, supporting him and cheering him on. Almost two years later, I am now walking up to three miles every day, but because of the pandemic, I cannot really enjoy getting out and doing much of anything.

While the ECMO life support I was on gave me the time I needed to get to the surgery I needed, it did not come without its side effects.

One of the side effects of ECMO is Femoral Neuropathy. I primarily experience that in my right foot, but it affects both feet to a degree. It is hard to explain, but my right foot constantly has a tingling, pins and needles sensation. Some days are better than others. Along with that, there is also a sort of numbness. If you were to take a toothpick and poke at my foot, I cannot feel that. However, if you run your finger down my foot it creates an excruciating sensation. I do have full use of both feet, but the feeling in the left is dulled and the feeling in the right is almost nil. As I said, it is hard to explain.

I also had severe muscle deterioration from being in a hospital bed 24/7 for 54 days. I had to relearn how to walk, talk and even eat solid foods. My arms are still fairly weak and I had to return for another stint in PT for what they call "frozen shoulder". I had very limited mobility in both shoulders. As the muscles started to rebuild, they tightened to the point that I could barely lift my arms.

My memory also took quite a hit from the strokes. Thankfully, I have worked in Assistive Technology for the last 15 years, so it was second nature for me to identify my needs and come up with solutions. I use apps like Google Keep to create checklists of to-do items and reminders for things such as appointments and grocery lists. I have lists for groceries for example that we can all add to and then I can check them off as I get them. Before the heart attack, I was the person in the household primarily responsible for grocery shopping. My wife took it while I was recovering, but I have gone back to doing it. The way I see it, I want to do as much as I can and be as active as I can for as long as I can. I use a Live Scribe Pen and an Apple Pencil with my iPad to take notes and transcribe meetings. I also record voice notes on my phone. If I want to remember it, I have to write it down or record it in some way.

My short-term memory deficits have put a lot of stress on both my family and me. My kids do not always understand why Dad cannot remember what he said 5 minutes ago. Thankfully, they have not taken advantage of that too much! My memory deficits also cause some anger on my part, which has led to some heated exchanges between my wife and me.

I had to learn to give up control over many of the things that I had traditionally done within our family. Being the primary driver when we would go on trips, doing yard work, changing oil in the cars, home repairs, etc. I am able to do some of those things now, not that I should though!

My parenting style has not really changed, but I have had to limit many of the things I do. I cannot be out in the heat for long periods. I have to be careful not to do anything that would cause me to bleed because I am on blood thinners. I have to be mindful of the three daily times I have to take my meds (I take between 15-20 pills every day). I cannot do heavy lifting or exert too much.

My kids have somewhat adjusted under the circumstances. My

son has always been able to adapt to almost any situation. However, he does like to reflect on things. We have often had conversations about the way things were before the heart attack, or about what it was like for him while I was in the hospital, or when I first returned home.

My daughter is much more reserved, like her dad! However, I know it has taken a toll on her emotionally. She was with me when the heart attack happened. I woke up feeling nauseous, but we did not think much of it beyond that. We were on vacation, so everyone else went out for the day. Taylor and I stayed behind. Her mom told her to watch over me and to call if I got worse or needed anything. She has carried that with her ever since. She feels like she did not do enough, while I was trying to hide everything from her. What she did not realize is that I had already called my wife and they were on the way back to the house to take me to Urgent Care (we still never suspected a heart attack).

My daughter and I have since talked about this. I have had to reassure her that none of us knew what was happening at the time. When my wife told her to watch me and take care of me, and to let her know if I got worse, she meant like if I needed a bucket to throw up in or a Sprite to drink to get it for me. Had we known what was really going on, they would have never left the house and we would have called an ambulance. That has forever scarred her, thinking she did not know what to do or somehow did not do enough. To this day, she is still nervous whenever my wife leaves the two of us alone in the house or if she and I go out somewhere together. She is afraid that something will happen to me and she will not know what to do.

I try not to look to the past too much; I try to be a forward thinker. I know that what I have been through has significantly lowered my life expectancy. I know that some day in the near future, I will most likely have to go on the list for a heart transplant. My last echocardiogram (January, 2021) showed my Ejection Fraction (EF) was 31%. It will likely never get higher than that. Ejection fraction (EF) is the measure of how well the heart is pumping out blood and is used to diagnose and monitor Heart Failure. The ejection fraction for a normal heart ranges between 50 and 70 (from the website www.keepitpumping.com). I make it a point to do as much as I can now, while I still can.

Chapter 22

Greg
"My family has always been a great support system for me"

Greg with his son, Tyler, wife, Angel, daughters, Haylee, Amber, and Megan, and the family dog, Zoey.

At the age of 21, I was diagnosed with Becker's Muscular Dystrophy. Becker's is related to Duchenne's Muscular Dystrophy, but progresses much more slowly. Individuals with Duchenne's usually cannot walk by the age of 12 and the average life expectancy is 26. I am much older than that now. I had been having problems for years, but had never gotten a definite diagnosis. I was given an EMG and initially diagnosed as having Duchenne's. I then went to a specialist who told me I didn't have Duchenne's because, at my age, I couldn't have walked into the office. I had a muscle biopsy about 1990 that resulted in the Becker's diagnosis. I finally had a DNA test in 2019 that confirmed the Becker's diagnosis.

When I married, my wife and I had many discussions about whether we should have children. We knew my muscles would continue to deteriorate slowly over the years and I would be physically capable of doing less and less. In addition, Becker's is an X-linked recessive inherited disorder. Women are carriers who don't develop symptoms, although in later years they can have some issues. They can pass the condition on to their sons, however. We did research. We talked to doctors. Ultimately, we made the decision to go for it.

After the decision was made, I guess we kind of went crazy. We now have four children. Our youngest daughter is eleven. Our oldest daughter is 22 and in a Master's Degree program at Eastern Kentucky University (EKU). Our other daughter is 20 and is at the Jefferson Community and Technical College (JCTC). Our son, 17, will be a senior in high school. That's right. I have three kids driving now!

Becker's is a degenerative disease of the muscles. Curbs and steps have long been a problem for me. Nowadays, a two-inch curb is difficult. Still, I didn't start using a walking stick all the time until the last two years. Becker's can affect any muscle. Occasionally, although not commonly, it can affect the heart. When I was in my early thirties, I started thinking there might be something wrong with my heart because I had researched Becker's Muscular Dystrophy on the internet. I had to ask my doctors for an EKG just to get a baseline. After the test, they sent me immediately to a cardiologist. The EKG had shown an irregular heartbeat and rhythm. The lesson learned: you can't just let your doctors and your family members make your health decisions for you. You have to be your own advocate. You have to do your own research and sift through the information because there is a lot of misinformation out there.

In 2010, I found out about a conference in Chicago specifically concerning Becker's MD. My wife and I decided to attend. I met up with a doctor there who has followed me ever since. She had treated some individuals with the condition and was familiar with it unlike the doctors in Louisville. She was not as alarmed about the heart issues. She knew the sort of impact it was going to have. My heart issues were adequately controlled for many years. Still, beginning last year, I started having heart failure. I went to Northwestern University for treatment and spent several months there. I was put on the heart transplant list. During Christmas of 2019, they implanted a Left Ventricle Assist Device (LVAD). I went from level 2 on the transplant list (immediate need) to level 4. The LVAD will offload my heart and hopefully my pulmonary artery, which was working too hard to make up for the weakened heart muscle. I will need a transplant eventually. My symptoms have definitely increased over the years.

As infants, if my children were sick or having trouble breathing, my wife could take them out of the crib and walk with them. I could sit in a rocker and she could hand them to me. I could rock them to help them sleep. My wife says she always had a 'built-in baby holder' so she could get other things done or take a break. I was much less physically involved with my last two children than my first two when they were infants and toddlers. I just wasn't as capable.

I was a strict disciplinarian when they were small. I had to teach them to stay with me. I couldn't run to catch them if they got away. I had the fear that I wasn't going to be there for them. It was too dangerous. The earliest years of my children's lives were the toughest for me, but I was always able to hold my children.

After my children could walk and get around, I was able to be more involved with them. I always loved sports so I was coaching youth sports even before any of them could play. When they did become old enough, I would coach them. Baseball and softball were the hardest for me. Because of my balance, I could not throw or hit or catch a ball very easily. I couldn't really even get out of the way of a thrown or hit ball. I gave coaching those sports up early on because of the danger to myself. My favorite sport to coach was basketball. In the beginning, I could dribble, pass, and shoot with the kids, but eventually I needed a good assistant to demonstrate things. Once, I was coaching one of my daughter's teams. We were getting pounded and I called a time out. We were talking to the team about rebounding. One of my assistants decided to demonstrate blocking out. He used me as a subject in his demonstration without thinking and sent me sprawling across the floor in a gym full of people. He has never forgotten that and often tells me he couldn't believe he did it.

When I was coaching, I could tell that some parents felt I shouldn't be doing it, but no one said anything to me point blank. More recently, when I have started to spend more time in a wheelchair, it does feel different to me. It feels like people have a different view of me. It is hard to explain. It is like I am not viewed as capable. When I was young I received some teasing from kids about the way I walk and do things. I can't say that my kids have ever heard anything from other kids about their father. They have never said anything about it anyway.

I learned to work smarter at things instead of harder. You learn to make adaptations as you go along. My wife always wonders how I am able to bring the Christmas tree up from the basement by myself. I tell her, 'One step at a time.' For a while now, I have had trouble bending over to pick things off the ground. I have trouble straightening back up and it wears me out so I use grabbers a lot. I can see how assistive technology could have been very useful when my kids were little, but the expense of some of it can be prohibitive. Prices need to come down so it is more available for parents.

My family has always been a great support system for me. My kids will help me with chores and will bring me things, but I have some guilt associated with having them do a lot for me. I have had to ask them for help for many projects around the home, but they eventually learned to jump in and help without me asking. They know what I can't do for myself.

I have trouble rising from a seated position. When I sit at a table, I can use the table to lift me up. I never sit in the first row in any place because I need to use the row in front of me to get up. My kids help me up often. When we are walking together, they will watch the terrain in front of me and let me know of any holes or objects in the way.

About four years ago, I started using a scooter for long distances. You know, you take your kids to an amusement park and one of them decides they want to go back and do such and such. My internal response would be "oh, no, how am I going to do that?" So, I thought I should get a scooter or a power wheelchair. I got a power wheelchair from Project CARAT, Kentucky's assistive technology and medical equipment reuse program. It has been a good thing for me to have. I even walk the dog with it.

My wife and I addressed my disability with the children from a very young age. My second daughter would say I had 'muscular differty' so you know she was pretty young when we talked to her. We let them know how it impacted me and why Daddy couldn't do certain things. I would have to explain up front why I couldn't hike, why I couldn't go up the hill. They also knew I volunteered for a lot of muscular dystrophy fundraising events.

I think having a father with a disability has made my children more compassionate, more likely to recognize inequities. They easily notice when things are inaccessible. They question why a restaurant has to have a two-inch rise into the dining room, why is that necessary? That can even be a problem for the wait staff. My disability certainly affected my daughter's choice of a career, occupational therapy. She watched me make and adapt things to make possible for me to do what I needed to do. My second daughter is going into the nursing field.

I would tell people with disabilities thinking of becoming parents: don't not do it out of fear. I have flaws as a parent, I can overreact to things, I have done some things wrong, but that has nothing to do with my disability. Having a disability should not preclude anyone from being a parent and it won't preclude anyone from being a good parent either.

Chapter 23

Kimberly
Everything in Life
is a Roll of the Dice

Kimberly with her husband, Michael, son, Ian, and daughter, Sayer.

Editor's Note: The following definition of Von Hippel Disease is taken from the website of the National Institute of Neurological Disorders and Stroke (NINDS). "Von Hippel-Lindau disease (VHL) is a rare, genetic multi-system disorder in which non-cancerous tumors grow in certain parts of the body. Slow-growing hemgioblastomas -- benign tumors with many blood vessels -- may develop in the brain, spinal cord, the retinas of the eyes, and near the inner ear. Cysts (fluid-filled sacs) may develop around the hemangioblastomas. Other types of tumors develop in the adrenal glands, the kidneys, or the pancreas. Symptoms of VHL vary among individuals and depend on the size and location of the tumors. Symptoms may include headaches, problems with balance and walking, dizziness, weakness of the limbs, vision problems, deafness in one ear, and high blood pressure. Individuals with VHL are also at a higher risk than normal for certain types of cancer, especially kidney cancer."

I lost my sight when I was 14 to a rare genetic disease. The disease I have is called Von Hippel Lindau (VHL). It can affect many, many areas of the body, I think up to ten organs. It usually starts in the retina. When I was diagnosed in 1996, I showed all the symptoms, but nobody in my family had ever had it. The doctors tested my Mom and Dad and neither had the gene. The doctors didn't think it was possible for me to have VHL, but it ended up being a new mutation. Now they think as many as 20% of cases are new mutations. It raises the question, what is causing the mutation of this gene? That would be a great thing to know, wouldn't it?

When I was 10, I had surgery to remove a huge retinal tumor. It was the first of about 30-some operations to try to save my sight. By the time I was 14, the surgeries had caused retinal detachment and other things. I was told that VHL was probably the disease I had, but I was not given any guidelines nor told what it would mean for me. When I was 20 and in college, I started having terrible, terrible headaches and other pain. My mother got connected to the National Organization for Rare Disorders. We found out about research that led us to the National Institutes of Health (NIH) where they did verify that we needed to be watching things a lot closer.

I have had many, many more surgeries since then. The disease started causing tumors in lots of different places. I've had eight to ten brain surgeries. In 2016, I had a tumor on my spinal cord at C-2, the top part of the spinal cord. That's not a place you want them cutting into. That surgery left me without the ability to use my left arm or my hand. Yes, I couldn't type anymore. I had written a number of books by then, including some fantasy novels. Not being able to type kind of took all the fun out of writing. I think my creativity flows through my fingertips.

My surgery in 2016 was at Vanderbilt University in Nashville. I was in the hospital for a month relearning how to walk. I had to go into physical therapy. I had to relearn how to feed myself. I had to relearn virtually everything all over again. There was no cognitive disability at all. It was all physical and motor. I could still speak, but everything with the hands and the legs was affected. I still walk with a very, very pronounced limp.

My last brain surgery was in 2019. Apparently, the brain has ventricles. I did not know that. The tumor was in one of the ventricles through which spinal fluid flows. You don't want to monkey with spinal fluid. I had a very large brain tumor and I am still experiencing balance issues. Right now I have a kidney tumor and will be facing surgery for that eventually. This disorder has different levels of severity depending upon the individual. It's always different. I know people who are blind and I know people who've never had any sort of retinal surgery. I know people who've hardly had a problem at all. I know people who have battled with kidney issues and I know people who've never had a kidney issue.

I had learned how to have one disability, but when you have multiple disabilities, that is a whole other thing. I don't think I ever realized it, but it's not uncommon. There are a lot of people who have multiple disabilities.

Growing up, I didn't want to have kids. It just wasn't something I saw myself doing. That remained true until my husband, Michael, and I had been married for about eleven years. Up until that time, we did not want children. But our thinking changed and we decided to have kids. I was about 30. We knew that there was a 50% chance any children we had could have VHL.

There is something called pre-implantation genetic diagnosis. Eggs are harvested and the eggs that have the VHL gene are discarded. Only the eggs that are free from the gene are fertilized and implanted. I feel it very important here to say that this is not the route we chose to take. That is not a judgment on anybody else's decision. It is a very personal decision. There are lots of things, lots of factors that go into that. Just because I made one decision doesn't mean that I would condemn someone else for making a different decision. I certainly don't want to come off as saying "My way is the right way." It was the right way for us. That's all I can say.

We knew that our children might have VHL. I asked my mother, "What would you have done if you had known this was going to happen to me?" She told me, "I would have had you anyway, even though we have been through so much. I would not have chosen any differently." Anytime you have a child, there's a chance that child, either at birth or later, will have an illness, accident or disability. That is part of choosing to be a parent. It is like wearing your heart on the outside of your body. It just is. My husband and I decided that we could handle the VHL possibility. Medical science being what it is, we just decided to hope and pray that there would eventually be an easier treatment than surgery or even a cure.

I had my son when I was almost 33. Before getting pregnant, I talked to my doctor. Not that long ago, we might have been told not to have a child, but he just told me, given my history, I should have a C section. Natural childbirth would be too much. The intracranial pressure during childbirth for someone who's had a lot of brain tumors was not a good idea. So it was decided I would have a C section. I had one tumor that appeared to be growing that the surgeon wanted to take out before we proceeded with the pregnancy, just because they didn't want to be in a situation where we couldn't do surgery because of the pregnancy. Once that was done, I got pregnant, and we had our son, Ian. I had my next brain surgery when my son was 20 months old.

Our daughter, Sayer, followed in 2011. We decided we wanted a second child, mainly because we didn't want our son to be alone. I was an "only child" and I didn't want him to be an "only child." He did not particularly appreciate that decision when his sister came along, believe it or not.

My blindness made me freak out about things when I first got pregnant. For instance, I was convinced that I had to find a talking thermometer because I just knew that my baby was going to have a fever and I wasn't going to know it because I couldn't read the thermometer. My baby would die or have brain damage because I couldn't read a thermometer. Once I had my baby, it was not a problem. I can say right now that, by feeling one of my children, I can tell within an eighth of a degree what their temperature is. I don't really need a thermometer, but it's one of those things I just obsessed about.

My daughter did not talk for her first year, did not talk at all. I was concerned and called First Steps (Kentucky's early intervention program). She was really on the border of being eligible for services given her age and other things, but I think because they knew how important her talking was and how her just pointing at things would cause me problems, they pushed ahead to get services for her. With their help, she was talking in no time.

The simple feat of feeding a baby was wicked hard for me, being blind. It really was hard feeding a baby a spoonful of carrot or whatever. Fortunately, at that time, I still had full use of both hands. I kept one hand on my baby's face, dipped into the food with the other one, and just tried to get it in there. Sometimes you miss. Bath time always came after feeding. They learned to help Mommy really quick. "Why is Mommy so bad at this? I think I will just take over."

My daughter, although she was slow at talking, was quick at walking. She started walking at nine months old. I did not promote her early mobility at all. Not at all. And she was a climber, too. That gave me a whole new set of problems, but the problems continually change. For instance, my son, that little baby I fed, is now 12 years old. I'm constantly saying, "Turn it down!"

I couldn't read to my kids, but we could go to story time at the public library if I could get a ride with other moms. We would go to library story time and Ian got read to that way.

Baby gates, of course, were very important for us. Overall, we did a lot more child-proofing than I think other couples have to do simply because child-proofing is also blind-proofing. We're not going to have a lot of knickknacks and things sitting around the house for me to knock over anyway. Plug covers, cabinet locks and things like that were important. We were just really, really hyper vigilant about child proofing.

I was never able to take both of my kids anywhere by myself. It was impossible for me. Two kids were very, very hard. When it was just one kid, I had one of those little backpacks with a tether which people say are horrible, "you're putting your kid on a leash," but it worked for me. We developed code phrases which I still use. If I say, "here I am" or "Ian, sound off" then he knows he has to say, "here I am." To this day, they both know when we're in a store and I say "Sound off", they have to say, "Here I am." They know they will get in some serious trouble if they don't.

Because of my poor balance and lack of stamina, I use a wheelchair when we have extended outings, like the Nashville Zoo, which we recently visited. The kids fight over who gets to push Mommy. People have all the apps now on their phone that have these instructions you need to read. I could use speech on my phone, but I have kids for that now.

My husband has been such a huge help for me, always willing to do anything to assist. And not just as a babysitter. He thoroughly enjoys being involved with his children. Michael had to do some adjusting in terms of his job. Before the children, he had a good career in computer technology. After our son was born, he became a teacher at the school where our kids would eventually go to school. That enabled him to spend more time at home and enabled me to attend more school functions, but it did mean a cut in pay. We had to make that sacrifice; he took a lower paying job so that we could have more freedom. That trade-off is still something that many parents, particularly women, have to make, regardless of a disability. Parenthood can affect your career progress. It did my husband's because he wanted me to be able to be there for our kids. We could not move further away for his job either, just because I needed to be close to my mother since she helps a lot with the kids, like picking them up from school.

My own expectations of myself and trying to be what is quote, unquote, normal, were the biggest hurdles I had to overcome in parenting. I was so worried about telling my children that I couldn't see. When they're babies, they don't know; they can't figure it out. When I finally decided to tell my son that Mommy couldn't see, it was such a big overwhelming deal in my mind that he would view me differently. He absolutely did not care. Mommy was still Mommy. Nothing changed about how he did things. It was no big deal. He probably didn't even remember it the next day. My daughter, on the other hand, had a different response and this says something about her personality. She said to me one time, "Mommy, I'm very sorry you're blind." I said, "That's nice of you to say." And she said, "Because you can't see how beautiful I am." That is totally my daughter.

Parenting is hard no matter who you are. It is hard every day. It's emotionally hard. It's physically hard. It's taxing. It's hard for everybody. But it's very, very worth it. It changes your life; your whole lifestyle is different. But if you're ready to do that, then I don't think disability should ever stop someone from parenting.

I guess you could say it's harder if you are blind. I did have some fear that if I was bad at it, they, whoever "they" are, would come and take my baby away from me. I've heard that concern from other women with disabilities. I shared it. I think, as with so many things, the biggest enemy was myself, what I thought, my own fears, what people would think of me. I remember I was all torn up that I couldn"t drive. Public transportation in the small city where we live is virtually non-existent. My husband worked, but I decided to stay home with my son. I was worried I couldn't drive him to places like to the playground like my Mom did for me. I would stay up feeling guilty about that. He did not care because he did not know any different. It did not bother him. He was just as happy playing in the backyard or playing with Legos or whatever. I am probably one of the few parents who is looking forward to their children reaching driving age. When Ian turns sixteen, I'm going to have a driver at my disposal!

I have never let my disability stop me from doing anything. That includes being a parent. A disability gives you a different worldview and probably greater empathy. We definitely need more people with empathy and understanding. There's a lived experience that disabled people have, it's hard fought and it can take a lot of blood, sweat and tears. We've earned that lived experience and can pass it on to our children and share it with them. You have to tell your children how important it is to not judge others, to always be there with empathy, love and acceptance for other people.

As I mentioned earlier, I had to have extensive physical therapy after my surgery in 2016. For one thing, I didn't have any use of my left arm. I couldn't give my kids a two-arm hug any more. The therapy made it possible for me to do that. It was so wonderful to put both arms around them again. I really missed being able to hug them, to hug them good. I can do that now.

(Editor's note: One of Kimberly's two children has Von Hippel-Lindau Disease.)

Rare Disease Drama

By Kimberly Parsley

I have cancer
Finally
For real this time
In the kidney
No less

I've had tumors before
A brain tumor
"Was it benign?"
Another brain tumor
"Was it benign?"
Dismissive
Not a real tumor

I wear blindness like a badge of courage Isn't this enough?
What about this hand that won't type? Isn't it enough?
The limp, didn't you see me stumble in here?
Never enough.

But it was cancer this time
The real deal
And yet
Was it?
There was no radiation, no chemo
Why even be cancer at all?

This is my rare disease.
It attacks again and again and again
With velvet claws
Soft enough that people can withhold their tears A bullet dodged

This is my rare disease
Velvet claws rake
They scar
Again
And again
And again

Chapter 24

Jerry and Lee
Why We Decided
Not to Have Children

Jerry and Lee live in Bardstown, Kentucky

Jerry: I have retinitis pigmentosa (RP), a recessive inherited disorder. It is the leading cause of inherited blindness. There are a lot of versions of RP. In some people, it doesn't show up until they are in their forties and fifties. In others, like my younger brother, it can significantly affect your sight from birth.

I don't really remember when I first realized I was having trouble with my vision. My Mom and Dad must have started thinking something was not quite right when I was about five. I remember my Dad started giving me the "penny test" when I was about that age. He would throw pennies on the floor one at a time and tell me to find them. I had trouble doing it.

I went to the eye doctor when I was about six, but the doctor didn't know what I had. He prescribed glasses. When I started in grade school, the teacher put me in the front row so I could see the board. She soon noticed that I could see better, although certainly not well, without my glasses so we ditched the glasses. I was eventually diagnosed with RP at about the age of eight when my parents took me to the Lion's Eye Institute in Louisville

There was no history of the disease in either my mother's or my father's family before I was born. My parents had nine children in ten years (a good Catholic family of the fifties and sixties). Three of us have RP. Both of my parents obviously had the recessive gene. I was the second oldest of the nine siblings. The second child to be diagnosed was my brother Ronny, one of the middle children. The second youngest of us, my brother, Jeff, was the third child with RP. He had very low vision at birth. Unlike Ronny and me, he attended the Kentucky School for the Blind from the first through the twelfth grades.

In 1967, my two brothers with RP, two of our unaffected siblings, and myself went to Louisville for a study. It was a big deal for us. We were there for three days and two nights. We went for a variety of tests and they put us up in a hotel at night. That was our first experience in a hotel. Back home in Raywick (a rural community in Marion County, Kentucky, about 50 miles from Louisville), we still didn't have running water in our house. We had electricity and we heated the house with a wood stove, but no running water. Running water at the hotel was quite a big deal. Getting to order anything we wanted at restaurants was awesome.

I was able to attend regular public elementary school (grades one through eight at the time) and the first two years of public high school. I spent my last two years of high school at the Kentucky School for the Blind. I was losing my ability to read regular print and my vision was deteriorating faster. I would gradually lose all of my vision over time, but I still had light perception up until the age of 37 or 38. When I finally lost that and became totally blind, that might have been the hardest for me. I lost my independent mobility and my confidence with it for some time.

I grew up on a farm. It was a lifestyle that suited me. There is something about farming that gets in your blood. It's not a big money maker, but it was the life for me. After high school, I started farming, probably not the best career move, all things considered. I was a tobacco farmer and raised some cows and hogs. It got too dangerous for me when I was in my late twenties. I could still do most things, but I just had to be on a tractor. I didn't need to be. I am kind of surprised I didn't do harm to a niece or nephew or two.

I couldn't get a driver's license, of course, but at the time you didn't need a license to ride a motorized dirt bike in Kentucky. That's how I got around. I nearly killed myself a couple of times. Once I was following a couple of friends and they made a quick turn to avoid an old fence post. I didn't and my head met the fence post. I gave up the dirt bike about the time I gave up the tractor. Toward the end of my bike driving days, friends accused me of dragging my feet to stay on the road. This is an extreme exaggeration. The truth is I only drug my right foot and only in critical situations like when crossing a bridge near my home that had no guardrails.

I got married after high school. She was a city girl – she grew up in nearby Lebanon (the current population of Lebanon is just over 5,000). She was sighted. She could not physically have children. We struggled financially so we never considered adoption or fostering as an alternative. We were married for 11 years, until our late twenties. To be honest, I was not handling my vision loss well. I became kind of a jerk for a while.

After I had given up farming, I went to Western Kentucky University to take Computer Science courses. Then I went to the Arkansas Enterprises for the Blind to participate in an intense nine-month computer programming course. The course prepared you for jobs with the Internal Revenue Service (IRS). I met Lee, my future second wife, there. We have been together ever since, over 30 years. After finishing the course, the two of us moved to Newark, New Jersey, to work for the IRS. We stayed a year and then she came back to Kentucky with me. This country boy just couldn't adjust to Newark.

I have worked for non-profits and for the state in the years since. I also rehabbed and built houses with my uncle and maintained a number of rental properties for many years. When Lee and I retired a few years ago, we moved to a small farm near Bardstown. We dug and stocked a pond, we have planted fruit trees, and we raise feeder cows.

Lee: I was born and raised in St. Louis, Missouri. I had vision problems from birth. At first, they thought I was severely near-sighted and tried glasses to correct it, but glasses never worked. Then I was diagnosed with RP (I have two cousins with RP), but my vision never worsened. My symptoms, including night blindness, never really changed. I was misdiagnosed with RP well into my thirties and I have gotten different diagnoses since then. The most recent name for my disorder the eye doctor has given me is Optic Atrophy, but to be honest, I don't think they know what I have.

My father had a trash-hauling business in St. Louis. After that, he operated a gas station. After being robbed and shot on two separate occasions and experiencing heart problems, he retired and went on disability. My mother was a housewife, but she went to work after my father quit working. I had already gone away to college. She spent 30 years in the federal civil service working for the Army. I have two older brothers, neither of whom have a visual impairment.

I got my Bachelor's Degree in Sociology at Northeast Missouri State and my Master's in Counseling at Central Missouri State. After graduation, I couldn't find a job, so I enrolled in the IRS training program in Arkansas and met Jerry. The main problem I had with Newark was the high cost of living. I was more than happy to move to Kentucky where the cost of living was much lower. I went on to work for the Kentucky Office for the Blind for 27 years as a computer skills teacher before retiring. In the last few years, I have adjusted to country living quite well.

Jerry: It is very likely that Lee and I both carry the recessive gene for Retinitis Pigmentosa. It is obviously in both of our families. After we got together, the question soon came up about having children since there was a chance any kids we would have might have RP. We discussed it and ultimately decided we wouldn't have children.

For me, it wasn't just about the possibility of passing on RP. Ultimately, I just don't think I was mature enough to risk the possible pain of having children. I just didn't want to take a chance, not only that they might have RP, but that something else might happen to them. When I was still farming, a good friend of mine had a son that followed him everywhere on the farm from a very young age. When you are a farmer, you need help with many things, but you can't afford to hire anybody to help you. Neighboring farmers tend to trade off labor when they need it. My friend and I did that a lot and whenever I was working with him, his son was always around. When the boy was five, he was killed in a freak accident in the barn. He was playing on a piece of equipment called a grater blade and it accidentally fell over on him. It broke my friend's heart. I don't think he ever fully recovered. How could you? That had a huge impact on me. So many things can go wrong when you are raising children. I didn't think I could go through something like that.

Lee: I was never a person who felt I had to have a child. It was not something that was always in my plans or anything like that. I think I would have gone along with having children had Jerry wanted them, but not having them was acceptable to me, too.

Jerry: I had a great childhood. I can't imagine how it could have been any better. My parents were great parents. They never treated the three of us with RP any differently than our other siblings. They let us go and take our chances. They let us try anything. I can't imagine doing as good a job at parenting as they did.

Neither of my brothers with RP had natural children. My middle brother has step-children. My youngest brother with RP tried unsuccessfully with his first wife to have kids. They ended up adopting two children.

Deciding not to have children is not that unusual of a decision in this country anymore. The birthrate is declining and more people are making the decision not to have children at all. (Editor's note: the birthrate in the United States has declined from 24.268 births per 1,000 people in 1950 to 11.990 in 2020.)

Lee: We talked about adopting, but ultimately decided against it. We have always had so much going on we never stopped long enough to seriously consider it.

Jerry: Occasionally, I do wonder what it would have been like to have kids and, now, grandkids. Interestingly, I have over 20 nieces and nephews and over 20 great-nieces and great-nephews and none of them have RP. Some of them have had worse problems than that though. The dogs we have had have been enough responsibility for me.

Lee: I have always been a very practical person. I don't worry about hypotheticals. I don't have any regrets. We have a great life together. And our dogs have been great.

Chapter 25

Kevin
Eulogy for my Dad

Kevin's Dad in Tucson, Arizona, in the 1960s

My two brothers and I were raised by two loving, dutiful, and resourceful parents, even though one of them - my Dad - had a profound, life-altering, and highly visible disability. His condition - and how he responded to it - imbued me with unique sentiments and perspectives regarding all disadvantaged and differently-abled persons. This is that story, through his story.

Born in 1919, Dad grew up as a typical child during the 1920s. When he was in his pre-teen years in the early 1930s, he contracted osteomyelitis, probably due to a fall and a broken leg. This infectious disease attacks bones from the outside inwards and often afflicts the "long bones" of the limbs, plus the pelvis and the spine. Easily treated today by antibiotics, in the pre-penicillin 1930s, the only known treatment was to surgically remove the flesh above an infected site, then scrape and remove the surface of infected bone. The open wound would then be bandaged until skin grew back over the wound and the exposed bone.

My Dad, as a young teenager, was in a bed in a Louisville children's hospital for three years, during which he endured dozens of such surgeries. Once the infections finally abated, he was covered with many deep trenches, divots, and scars over his legs, pelvis, and one arm. He was also left with many atrophied muscles and fused, immovable joints in his knees, hips, lower back, and one elbow. In effect, his body was as straight and as stiff as a board, a condition sometimes dubbed "full-body ankylosis."

He retained strength and flexibility in his upper body and arms except for the one immovable elbow. He taught himself to "walk" with crutches, swinging himself pendulum-like forward between his "sticks," as he called them. For staircases with handrails, he taught himself to climb stairs - albeit slowly and backwards - lifting himself one step at a time. He learned to clamber onto public transit buses - before hydraulic lowering or lifts. He attended high school for several years, taking courses in mechanical drafting.

That drafting training - plus the massive World War II mobilization of young men - opened a position for him at a Louisville industrial equipment manufacturer. He built his skills and value to the company and rose through the ranks. Ten years later he met and married our mother in the early 1950s. They immediately birthed three boys, one year apart, starting with me in 1954.

As a toddler and preschooler, I don't recall thinking of my Dad as all that different from other dads - sort of in the way one sees that some folks have brown hair and others, black or blonde. Before my birth, he bought the family's first car, installed a hand control for gas and brakes, and commuted to work like other dads. He would return from work happy to see us tykes and loved spending time with us evenings and weekends. Due to his flat, stiff body, he provided us little ones with the biggest lap on the planet. We spent hundreds of hours there or on the arms of his chair, as we jointly flipped through the pages of Time Life coffee table science books about dinosaurs, evolution, archeology, or astronomy. He helped us learn to read there, pre-kindergarten.

All through this toddler and preschooler period, he would drive us to public venues for shopping or ice cream or restaurants or whatever. By perhaps age seven, as we all walked together through these public places, I began to recognize the many surrounding gazes fixed upon Dad.

Some onlookers, I'm sure, were simply curious. But many had the look of pity in their eyes. This was most often revealed when they would avert their gaze, embarrassed, if I - even as a child - caught their eye. If I ever felt anger or resentment towards those onlookers, I don't recall it. But I do recall never being embarrassed myself for my Dad. It gradually dawned on me that he had had to endure those gazes of pity all day long, every single day, for all of his adult life. And yet he soldiered on, with quiet confidence, to pursue his dreams.

Those dreams were mainly: first, supporting his family, and second, advancing his career to better support his family. So, his career took us to Chicago in the late 1950s, to Tucson in the early 1960s, then back to Louisville in the late 1960s. With every move, he provided us with a large, comfortable home, a private school education, and, at one point, an in-ground swimming pool. When I was in college, he was a senior manager in that same manufacturing firm that had - decades earlier - hired him as a draftsman. By the time he had retired from that firm at age 80, he had served as its Chairman of the Board.

The unsung hero in the above narrative and the equal partner in Dad's success with his family and career was our Mom. Over other suitors, she chose to marry a man on crutches, then have three kids with him. She embraced countless additional burdens to compensate for Dad's limitations - everything from household maintenance to childcare to any special treatment or attention that Dad might need. Perhaps hardest of all, she had to help raise three rambunctious boys into men. Finally, moving through life with him, she endured the same gazes from strangers as did Dad. Quietly, modestly, and in the background, she finessed all these challenges until illness took her life in 1994. Her name was Mildred Drummond McAdams.

Almost 20 years later, Dad died peacefully, at home, surrounded by family, at age 94. And his name was Robert Pope McAdams, Jr.

Kevin (far right) with his Dad and two brothers, Robin (left) and Marc, mid-2000s

Chapter 26

Alison
Disability and Marriage Rules
Originally Published on July 27, 2018
Reprinted with Permission

Al and Alison

We are in the midst of wedding season. Weddings are generally beautiful affairs where two people commit to one another, announce their love to the world, and celebrate their relationship with family and friends. I attended two weddings this year, one for my cousin in Ohio, and another where a long-time friend of Al's got married. They both were beautiful and celebratory, and I had a great time. Both weddings had a priest presiding over the ceremony and got a marriage license prior to the event. Upon their wedding days, those licenses were signed by the correct representatives and they became legally connected with guaranteed shared rights.

The financial cost of marriage on SSI

Most people who are or become disabled prior to marriage find that they cannot afford the costs of getting married. I am not just, or even primarily, talking about the financial costs of a ceremony (which can vary dramatically and can be planned with budgetary considerations). I am talking about financial benefits from the federal and state government. Most social welfare programs, including SSI are based on financial need. As a single person, only your income and assets are considered in your application for these programs.

While SSI does provide some income to survive on, and SNAP benefits to help purchase food, the most important service they offer is Medicaid, which covers much, sometimes all, of the medical needs of a person with a disability. Those costs are the primary concern for a person with a disability and, if they are married, their spouse's income and assets are also considered, which can easily lead to ineligibility.

If both members of the couple are disabled, there are also ramifications – asset limits are for individuals, or a couple. The amount of assets that a married couple is allowed to have and remain eligible for SSI is $3,000. Every single person can have up to $2000 in assets. Not only could one person lose their benefits, but both people can be denied for having the same exact amount of assets as they had prior to marriage.

If two people on SSI are not married, they can live together and each would have access to just under $2,000 of assets and be fine. However, the minute they are married, if their assets are over $3,000, they BOTH are no longer eligible for benefits. They no longer get food stamps, they no longer get a monthly check, and, most importantly, they no longer have Medicaid to manage their healthcare. So the only intelligent thing to do is to not get married.

The financial cost of marriage on SSDI

SSDI is based upon individual work history and has fewer asset-related limitations. If the only benefit you receive is SSDI, which provides Medicare coverage and a monthly check, marriage isn't financially impossible, but access to any of the financially-based programs (pretty much all other social welfare programs) may be more challenging. You will need to provide information about both your and your spouse's assets for all future requests of any sort.

While some programs discuss household values (which would affect you and your partner from the moment you live together), sometimes only individual assets are considered for supports. You can apply as an individual for supports on SSDI if you are unmarried, but if you are married your spouse's assets are always considered. Also, if for any reason your partner later needs assistance they will have their application process potentially impeded by your benefits and assets.

As I mentioned above, SSI and other programs will consider spousal assets. As an example, I know somebody who is on SSI benefits and is married to a person on SSDI. Because they are married, she only remains eligible for SSI if they live separately and maintain separate households. If she wanted to live with him, she would lose her Medicaid coverage, but their marriage would not make her eligible for his Medicare.

Laws on healthcare

If these programs only provided money, I would not be as concerned. However, currently, the United States is in a health-care crisis. SSDI provides Medicare coverage and SSI provides Medicaid coverage. Often these are the only health care coverage options we receive. We only receive the coverage if we are currently receiving benefits. So, if by getting married we lose benefits, we also lose our healthcare.

People with disabilities, by definition, are more apt to need health care than anybody else. We have medications and medical care needed to maintain our quality of life, and in many cases, simply to stay alive. If our spouses have health care, by marrying we are eligible to join their plan, but that often comes with increased financial costs and assumes the spouse has health care in the first place. This also places those of us with disabilities in a place of dependency on our partners. The right to theoretically use a spouse's possible benefits is generally not as useful as having a source of health insurance that isn't dependent on employment status.

Laws on medical decisions

Also, one of the rights that comes with a legally recognized marriage is legal recognition as next-of-kin to your spouse. This is extremely important in the case of severe injury (which may cause a disability), as it is the next-of-kin who often makes health-related decisions if the person who sustained the injury is unable to make their own medical decisions. Also, in the case of a chronic and worsening condition, there is a high risk of the disabled person being unable to make some of the decisions in an emergency. When a person is unmarried, legally their next-of-kin tends to be their parents or children, unless otherwise specified in a living will or similar document. This means that for a person with a disability, the decision not to marry can also have substantial ramifications, especially if the relationship between their partner and their family is challenging, or the family and disabled individual are in disagreement about the best course of treatment.

My situation

Al and I have elected not to get married, as while my SSDI benefits aren't under extreme risk, we wanted to maintain my options for additional assistance if I needed it. For some time, for example, I was supported by the New Jersey Workability program, which allowed me to have Medicaid benefits while employed. This cut down on my medical expenses, as Medicaid generally covers the remainder of medical costs (while Medicare covers 80%) and allowed me to be eligible for additional supports like a home health aide, which I did take advantage of at one point.

If Al and I had been married, getting on the workability program would have required jumping through additional hoops and would have made Al's work income a potential issue if he found a better paying job. To protect him from fear of preventing me from getting all the support I needed, we elected not to get married.

Now, we are in a very different situation. Al is unemployed, no longer eligible for unemployment benefits, and looking for work. He isn't sure what or how much work he can physically handle due to the constant pain he is in. He has a spotty work history caused by events outside of his control, including the great recession in 2008 and a brain injury in 2012 that kept him unable to contemplate working for over a year. Due to this, he is ineligible for SSDI, which requires full-time employment for 5 of the previous 10 years (he has more than enough points to be eligible for retirement benefits). His only recourse is to apply for SSI to help him through as he looks for opportunities and contemplates hip replacement surgery – which should help in the long-term, but will temporarily worsen his challenges.

If we were married, my benefits and assets would make his eligibility for SSI impossible. As things stand, he was rejected based on asset calculations the first time around. I am applying for SNAP and LIHEAP benefits for us while we wait, as my income is too high for me to be eligible for either program as a household of one but low enough for our household of two (which we are by virtue of living in the same apartment) to be eligible for those benefits.

Conclusion: Disability and marriage rules

Weddings are wonderful activities and ways to celebrate a couple's love and commitment to one another. For most people, the benefits of marriage outweigh the costs. There are many government sanctioned benefits and protections that people who are not disabled receive when their marriage is legally recognized. Same-sex couples have fought for these rights, and am I glad that currently those rights are protected.

For people with disabilities, however, the equations look very different. Our lives and the quality of life we can enjoy is rooted in our ability to access health insurance. When they are asset-based, like SSI, the decision whether or not to marry is literally life-or-death.

There are people out there whose marriage has forced them to live separately in order for one of them to have SSI and loving couples who cannot have their love legally recognized due to fear of losing their benefits. With all of the discussion that has been coming up lately about marriage and marriage rights, I ask you to consider the ways in which people who are or become disabled are impacted by their marital status.

Editor's note: Alison Hayes is a coach and educator. She runs a blog, www.thrivingwhiledisabled.com, where she discusses practical solutions to common challenges to help others with disabilities to thrive!

More about the "Marriage Penalty"

The following information was provided by Donna Mundy, Certified Work Incentive Coordinator (CWIC) with the Center for Accessible Living in Louisville, Kentucky.

The effect on benefits of marrying can differ greatly from individual to individual, dependent upon many factors. If both parties in a marriage have SSI, they do have time to spend-down their assets to get under the $3,000 limit, but if they are over the limit with assets and resources after the time limit, their SSI and Medicaid would discontinue. ABLE accounts can be great in helping people to get under the limits. In some states, even if an individual gets SSI, s/he has to apply separately for Medicaid. In Kentucky (and any so-called 1634 states), if an individual is eligible for SSI, s/he likely has met all the income restrictions and are automatically eligible for Medicaid. There are protections like 1619(b) which can help.

States can differ greatly. If a person with SSDI gets married and the SSDI benefit is high enough, it may cause a problem marrying someone with SSI or if they apply for SSI in the future. With both SSI and Medicaid programs being payers of last resort, they do want you to spend your own money first. If someone with SSDI has significant resources, assets, etc. it makes sense that s/he would provide support for his/her spouse. As for as SNAP, MSP programs, TANF, they do look at households and sometimes that is better for the individual and sometimes it is not.

There is also something called "holding out as married." In this situation, a couple present themselves to the community in which they live as married but they are not legally married. There are some agencies who will look at people who have been together for years as a couple and other agencies who do not as they know it might cause financial hardship.

A person who marries someone with a Title II (Social Security Disability Insurance (SSDI), Childhood Disability Benefit (CDB), or Disabled Widow Benefit (DWB) benefit does not become eligible for Medicare simply by being a spouse. They have to meet their own requirement, like being 65 years old or having a disability with the 24-month waiting period.

Chapter 27
A Look Back at the Carney Decision
By Dave Matheis

Originally published in the May/June 1993 issue of *The Disability Rag ReSource Magazine* Reprinted with Permission

When Mary-Lynne Fisher speaks before groups and large audiences today, she is still introduced as "the attorney who handled the Carney case." This is nearly 16 years after she obtained what was a landmark decision from the California Supreme Court. Interviewed by telephone recently, Fisher looked back on what was a truly precedent-setting case. As she puts it, "as far as I know, the Carney decision remains the leading decision in favor of a person with a disability in a private matter." But the decision had wider applications than that. It is commonly used by family lawyers who know little, if anything, of how disability was involved. Just what was the Carney decision and what were its implications?

In 1972, Bill Carney lived in New York with his wife and two infant sons. His marriage crumbling, Carney took the boys, Will and Ed, to Phoenix and joined the Marines. His wife followed to try a reconciliation, but the attempt lasted only a month. She was soon back in New York with her sons. It was not long before she notified her estranged husband that he would have to send more support money or she was going to turn the boys over to foster care. Carney immediately went to New York and took them with him to Memphis, where he was in school at a Marine base. In 1972, his wife relinquished custody in a written agreement.

Life in the Marine Corps can conflict severely with single parenthood, especially when the children involved are only one and two years old. The Corps "encouraged" Carney to take a hardship discharge. He joined the Army Reserve and moved on to Washington state.

On August 17, 1976, while on active duty with the Reserve in California, Carney was in a jeep accident. He suffered a spinal cord injury and became quadriplegic. In May of 1977, while undergoing rehab, he finally filed for divorce in California from his wife who was still in New York. At first, it looked as if his wife would settle things amicably, but she changed her mind and decided to fight for custody of her sons. She had not seen them in five years.

Mason Rose, an attorney from Beverly Hills, represented Carney in his divorce case. The custody fight went to court in August of 1977, one year after the accident. As Carney now remembers, the judge's attitude during the trial betrayed the final outcome. The judge was overly preoccupied throughout the proceedings with Carney's inability to play sports and engage in other physical activities with his sons. Despite the testimony of a psychologist, Dr. Jack Share, that the children had a warm and loving relationship with their father, accepted his authority, and had adjusted very well to his disability, the decision was a foregone conclusion.

The judge awarded custody to the mother, essentially agreeing with her argument that her husband's disability was a sufficient change in circumstances to justify a change in custody. He ruled that, because of his disability, Carney could not have a normal relationship with his children. The mother, despite the fact that she had gone five years without seeing her sons, would make a better parent than someone in a wheelchair. Adding insult to injury, the judge ignored a California law that would have enabled him to order an automatic stay before the decision was enforced. He allowed the mother to take the children on a plane to New York that very day. Carney would not see his boys again for nearly four years.

Carney immediately appealed. Mary-Lynne Fisher, then an attorney with the Western Law Center for the Handicapped, handled the appeal. The next step was the Appellate Court. Things there did not go any better. As Fisher tells it now, it was obvious from the moment the proceedings began that the judges had made up their minds based on the briefs. The oral arguments were useless. The Appellate Court upheld the lower court's ruling.

Carney next appealed to the California Supreme Court. According to Fisher, the prospects initially looked dim. The Supreme Court first had to be convinced to give the case a hearing. At the time, the Court was split over the recent appointment of a new Chief Justice by Governor Jerry Brown. It was volatile and unpredictable. Surprisingly, however, the judges agreed to hear the case.

This time the arguments made by Carney's side worked. Amazingly, the politically divided court ruled unanimously in Carney's favor. In August of 1979, the California Supreme Court overturned the lower court's decision. The Court ruled that the essential functions of parenting are to educate, guide and nurture children, and not merely to meet physical needs. The decision said that the lower court had relied on "outdated stereotypes" concerning parenting and people with disabilities. Disability alone was not a sufficient change in circumstance to warrant a change in custody.

Fisher believes that the Court's willingness to hear the case and their final decision were partially due to the behind-the-scenes work of a research attorney on the Court's staff who was a polio survivor.

As mentioned earlier, the Carney decision was one of lasting significance. "For the first time," Fisher says, "a court recognized that people with disabilities are real people who can function in and enjoy relationships." The persistence of one man paved the way for other people with disabilities to follow. Outside of the issue of disability, however, the decision is often used by many family attorneys today because it placed the burden of proof squarely upon the parent seeking a custody change.

Carney's fight to get his children back was not over, but it was mostly downhill from there. With the original decision now thrown out, the custody trial had to be retried. After Carney assured the court that he would take care of his children's physical needs by hiring live-in assistants with his veterans' benefits, he was awarded permanent custody.

Carney remembers that court proceeding well. By the end of the day on April 1, 1981, most of the arguments in the case had been heard. The judge would rule the next day after closing comments from both sides. Carney was leaving the courtroom in an apprehensive mood, which he had become quite accustomed to, when one of the bailiffs asked him if he was ready to get his kids back. Carney took that as a vote of confidence from someone who must have known the judge and his previous rulings well. The next day, Carney's sons were once again living with him.

After the decision, the boys went with Carney to his home in Las Vegas where he had moved in 1979. The case had received much publicity and soon became the subject of a made-for-TV movie starring Ray Sharkey as Carney and Betty Buckley as Fisher. It was broadcast around Christmastime. Life settled down after that. The home Will and Ed grew up in was a rambunctious one, always filled with their friends. Carney says now that he sometimes feels like he raised twelve sons instead of two. In the early eighties, both boys decided they no longer wanted to return to New York during the summer to visit their mother.

Will is now 23. He attends the University of Nevada at Las Vegas hoping to be a physician. He is engaged to marry. Ed is 22. He is currently living in Florida, less certain of his future and somewhat more bothered by his past.

In 1989, the Carney case was featured on an anniversary edition of the "20/20" television show. It was the third time the case had been featured on the show. Carney says he and his sons will get the TV movie out occasionally and have a good laugh at its melodramatic inventions and disability stereotypes. In the film Carney turned to drink temporarily and was prepared to give up during one low point in the struggle. In actuality, Carney stopped drinking completely many years before and never once thought about giving up. If he had lost at the California Supreme Court, he was ready to go on to the next step.

Mary-Lynne Fisher, the attorney who guided the appeals to a successful conclusion, left the Western Law Center in 1980, anticipating cutbacks in legal services. She became a clinical law professor at the Loyola Marymount University Law School. Later, she was named clinical law director at the school and, while in that position, was instrumental in moving the Western Law Center onto the campus. In 1989, she went into private practice in Glendale, California. She recently became a Certified Family Law Specialist.

Bill Carney gives full credit for the success of his appeal before the California Supreme Court to Fisher. He feels that without her involvement he never would have won. Although she did not handle his second custody trial, he also believes her work in support of that case was instrumental in obtaining a favorable decision.

Fisher remembers an ironic incident that took place that day in August of 1979 when the Supreme Court heard the case. After they had delivered their arguments in the morning, the Carney legal team was pleased and optimistic. They went downstairs to eat in a courthouse restaurant in a nearly euphoric mood. The group included Fisher, Mason Rose, Deputy Attorney General Sam Overton, who had filed an amicus brief in the case, and Marilyn Holle, an attorney who was then the legal director of the Western Law Center (Carney did not attend the legal arguments at the Court). Rose and Overton were wheelchair users. The restaurant was divided into two sections, one accessible, one not. The accessible section was closed between the lunch and dinner rushes and the restaurant employees refused to open the accessible part which effectively meant the group could not eat at the restaurant. Rose protested loudly and vehemently until the employees agreed to open the accessible area. Fisher says of the incident now, "It just goes to show that the struggle is never over. There is always one more battle to fight."

An Excerpt from the Carney Decision

The following is excerpted from the decision of the California Supreme Court overturning a lower court's decision in the divorce proceedings of William T. Carney and his wife on August 7, 1979.

"Contemporary psychology confirms what wise families have perhaps always known – that the essence of parenting is not found in the harried rounds of daily carpooling endemic to modern suburban life, or even the doggedly dutiful acts of "togetherness" committed every weekend by well-meaning fathers and mothers across America. Rather, its essence lies in the ethical, emotional and intellectual guidance that the parent gives to the child throughout his formative years, and beyond. The source of this guidance is the adult's own experience of life; its motive power is parental love and concern for the child's well-being; and its teachings deal with such fundamental matters as the child's feelings about himself, his conduct, and his goals and priorities in life. Even if it is true, as the court herein asserted, that William cannot do "anything" for his sons except "talk to them and teach them, to be a tutor," that would not only be enough – contrary to the court's decision – it would be the most valuable service a parent can render."

Chapter 28

Tom and Junie
The Veteran and His Family

Tom and Junie with their children

Tom: I spent 15 years in the Navy. I was the first person in my extended family to serve in the military since World War II. I chose the Navy for two reasons: I hated camping and I couldn't outrun a bullet. I knew I could swim and tread water so I figured a might have a chance to fight off a shark.

In July of 1994 while on a weekend getaway to Victorville, California, my life was changed in an instant. While trying to teach our nine-year-old daughter how to dive, I inadvertently struck the bottom of the five-foot end of a swimming pool and was knocked unconscious. My wife was pregnant with our fourth child and had stayed in the hotel room so it was just me and our three girls, ages nine, five and three. Our oldest daughter, Kayleigh, pulled me to the shallow end and flipped me onto my back, probably saving my life that day (she still loves to remind her siblings of that fact from time to time).

Junie, my wife, came down a few minutes later and discovered what had happened. She jumped in the pool and began calling for help. I was found to be comatose and unresponsive by the paramedics I required resuscitative measures by the pool side, during the ambulance ride and again upon arrival in the emergency room My wife likes to joke that I knocked on heaven's door three times and they still wouldn't let me in. OUCH! I had sustained a significant closed head injury, crushed C5 and C6 vertebrae, and a near drowning. It was estimated that I was unconscious in the pool for eight to ten minutes. I spent a total of ten months in the hospital which included five months in a halo and six weeks on a ventilator. In July of 1995, I was medically retired from the Navy and moved my family to Kentucky to start a new life.

Junie (Tom's wife): At Tom's retirement, his Navy buddies presented him with a diving trophy. The plaque read:

> **Victorville 1994**
> **Shallow Water Diving Competition**
> **CPO Division**
> **Honorable Mention**
> **HTC (SW) Vallandingham**

I guess they didn't feel he did well enough to place. It still makes me laugh. It was the first example of the (sometimes dark) humor that would become part of our lives.

I see now that it was God who gave us the strength to keep moving forward one day at a time.

Tom: I had grown up in Kentucky on a farm near Cynthiana in Harrison County. We had planned to retire to there from the military anyway. The plan had been to serve my 20 years and buy a farm back in Cynthiana. Despite my injury, we stuck with that plan.

My wife had our fourth child in December of the year of the injury, our son, right in the middle of my ten months of rehab. Six months later, we added two more kids to our family. My wife's sister died and her two sons, aged 15 and 12, came to live with us permanently. They became members of our family, not just nephews who were living with us, but two more sons for us and two more brothers for our four children.

Junie: When our nephews became a part of our family, we said to each other, "What are we going to do with six kids?" We agreed, "Keep them busy." That's why we bought the farm.

Tom: Our first effort to buy a farm was unsuccessful. A friend of mine told me he would sell us a farm, but when we were ready, he decided I wouldn't be able to able to keep it up because of my disability and withdrew the offer. Undaunted, we kept looking and eventually found a small farm to buy. It was 25 acres (later, the state decided they needed five of the acres for a by-pass). We never had any trouble keeping it up and it has been a working farm from the very start.

We grew tobacco and hay on the farm. I grew up on dairy farm. When I was in high school, I milked 150 head of cattle every day and I knew I didn't want to have anything to do with that again.

I did what I could and everyone in the family pitched in to do what I couldn't. Other relatives helped out when we needed it – cousins, brothers-in-law. I hired help occasionally.

Junie: I hated stripping tobacco. We stripped the tobacco in the garage because the stripping room in the barn was not accessible for Tom. It was the only way Tom could work alongside us. It was always important that we work with him; not just for him. It was one of many ways to teach the children the importance of adapting and problem solving.

One day Tom looked at me and said, "You could learn how to drive a tractor, you know." I replied, "Yes, I know. I don't want to." That's how I adapt and problem solve.

Tom: We also raised Belgian draft horses for show for a few years. We loved doing that. We traveled the country showing the horses and we had a great time. My father modified a sled with a ramp so I could drive the horses, but I never drove them in the shows. That was our oldest son's job.

There was one time when the horses pulled me out of my wheelchair and dragged me for a distance. They had been trained not to run away so they just went to the corner of the pasture, stopped and dropped me in a big pile of horse manure.

Junie: We laugh about that now, but I was scared to death when it happened. I thought he might have gotten hurt, but he was fine other than needing a bath. Tom was always able to laugh at himself.

Tom: One day, our horse barn burned down. None of the horses were in it, fortunately, but we decided to give up the horses after that. I had them shipped to my father's farm in Illinois. My youngest son, Tommy, he is 26 now, he keeps wanting us to get more horses, but we have gotten too old for that.

My family adjusted easily to my disability. The kids did real good with it. They accepted my limitations. The family knew they would have to help me with things. My wife learned to do things around the farm and would teach the kids what to do. I taught them as much as I could. I taught them how to fix mechanical things, a skill that has served them well. The kids learned to work very hard. We taught them how to work and we taught them how to have fun.

Junie: It took a lot of hard work, patience, a good sense of humor – (dark humor, like I said before), and deep faith. And consistency. Tom never let any depression show. He never showed self-pity. He never quit.

Tom's disability helped us. We had to come together to get the work done. We put in lots of hours and I think it drew everyone closer. His disability became a natural part of our lives. We did everything together. We went everywhere together. We still go on vacations together. Our oldest is nearly 40 and our youngest is 26. We have eleven grandchildren.

I think having a father with a disability made the kids more sympathetic and conscientious. It made them better people. Since they had to help out so much when they were young, they grew up to be confident adults.

Tom: My disability is just part of who I am for my kids. They really don't remember me any other way. My youngest, who was born six months after my accident, liked to sleep with me when he was young. When he was four or five, we were lying in bed one night when he spotted the softball trophies I had won while in the Navy. He asked me what they were for and I told him a won them for playing softball. He said, "Did Mom push you?"

Junie: Another time, our youngest son saw a framed picture of Tom and I in Hawaii, taken four months before Tom's accident. He said, "That's you Mommy, but who is that man with you, your boyfriend."

Tom: I was once a part of a program called "Everybody Counts' in the elementary schools here in Harrison County. The program was designed to introduce the kids to people with different disabilities. I would visit schools to talk about my disability. The kids loved the lift in my truck. When I am around town, I still get a lot of people who tell me they remember me being at their school many years before.

I had fair use of my two arms until a few years ago. I had a stroke in 2017 and it left my left arm useless. I can move it, but I really can't do anything else with it. My right arm still functions, but I can't drive any more. Since my accident, I had been able to drive with hand controls, but not now. I had to switch from a manual wheelchair to a power wheelchair. My son-in-law takes care of the farm now. He raises corn.

Our children have grown up to be fine people. Four of them graduated from the University of Kentucky and one from Morehead State University. Our oldest, Jim, served 12 years as a Navy Seal. He is married with two children and lives and works in Franklin, Tennessee. Our second oldest, Jacob, served five years in the Navy. Jacob has one child and he and his family live and work in Louisville. Our youngest son, Tommy, works for the Kentucky Farm Bureau and is currently looking for a farm of his own.

Kayleigh, our oldest daughter (and my lifesaver) is married with three children. Kayleigh married a farmer, something she said she would never do. Jordin is married with three children. Taylor, our youngest daughter is married with two children. She also married a farmer. All three of our daughters live and work in Cynthiana.

There have been many blessings that have resulted from my accident. My wife and I believe we are closer to God and our children because the daily challenges we all faced together. We have remained extremely close as a family and we are very proud of all our children. There is strength in our weaknesses.

I just got a new stand-up wheelchair. None of the kids or grandkids have seen it yet. I can't wait to see the looks of my grandchildren when they see me stand up.

*   *   *   *

Editor's Note: Tom and Junie's kids wanted to contribute to their parents' story. What follows are their comments, from the oldest child to the youngest.

Jim: It's very difficult to pick just one memory of Tom. I have dozens of stories, most of which are probably not fit for print. So, what I would like to share is how my time with him shaped who I am.

Lesson #1: Never feel sorry for yourself, and, if you do, keep it to yourself. Tom was never one for self-pity and most would gladly afford him the opportunity to feel sorry for himself, but he never did. Or at least he never let us kids see it. One day he convinced us he could work his draft horses on his own and all he needed was for us to hook the horses to a thousand-pound steel sled, drive his wheelchair on to the sled, and strap his hands to the reins using cornhuskers he bought from the Amish. We gave in and did as he asked. For about the first 30 minutes, it went well and we were all super proud of ourselves., it wasn't too long before the horses became agitated and came unhooked from the sled, but not unhooked from Tom. In a split second, he was flying out of his chair and being drug across the field. He went about 30 feet before the cornhuskers broke, but it was the funniest thing we had ever seen (see Lesson #2). Tom didn't lay there and feel sorry for himself, but said, "Get over here and get me back on that sled." Fortunately for us, Junie stepped in and put an end to that experiment.

Lesson #2: Laugh, it's the key to coping with shitty situations. Everything was hard for Jacob and me growing up as teenagers without our Mom or Dad. But Tom stepped up and made the best of it. Tom and Junie took us in and never once did we feel like a burden. I am certain it had to feel that way some time and could easily be described as a "shitty situation." Our solution to deal with it was too laugh. Laugh at each other. Laugh at Tom. Laugh at eight people in a 1,500 square foot house. We laughed more as a family than probably any family in the world. What else could you do? Dead mother, orphaned kids, paralyzed 33-year-old-man, newborn baby, six kids, etc. It could have been perceived as an absolute nightmare, but Tom ensured we all make the best of it and we did it through laughter. Nothing was off the table. No one was safe from being made fun of or being the center of attention for a while. It truly was an amazing experience.

Lesson #3: Life is about choices. Not a lot of people realize this, but Tom and Junie took us in well before our mother died. I can remember driving to Cincinnati a few times a week to visit my terminally ill Mom at the hospital before she died, about an hour drive. You would expect me to have negative memories of those drives, but I remember those drives very fondly. That is where Tom imparted his wisdom, where he became a father to us. Bottom line he was dealt a crappy hand, but he didn't let it get him down. How could we sit there and feel sorry for ourselves? He wasn't about to let that happen and those drives were where he would talk to us about life. He was great at talking "to you" and not "at you." Life is the summation of your choices. You could make good choices and have a good life or you could make bad choices and have a bad life, it was up to you.

I have used these three simple life lessons to help me get where I am. I try to impart them to my children. Tom is an amazing man and I feel very fortunate to have grown up around him.

Jacob: Growing up with Tom and Junie was probably what kept me from being a degenerate. I learned so much from them, but the biggest thing was not feeling sorry for myself. Our father more or less abandoned us before I can really remember. He would show up every few years to say hi but that was about it. I was 11 or 12 when my mom passed. Tom and Junie took us in without hesitation because that is what you do for family. With everything they had on their plates, four kids (one an infant) and the fact that Tom was suddenly a quadriplegic, they could have easily said they couldn't handle it and not a single person would have questioned it or had the slightest bit of judgement towards them. But they didn't. Instead, they opened their lives and home to two boys and treated them just like their own.

Growing up I remember Tom always telling me things that didn't click at the time, but are now fundamentals for how I live my life. I was told that "If something is worth doing, it's worth doing right" and that was instilled in me with a strong work ethic. But one thing Tom told me when I was younger was "No matter how bad you think your life is, someone else has it way worse. So be thankful for what you do have." Looking back, that one thing has stuck with me more than anything else. Tom didn't just tell us to not feel sorry for ourselves, but showed us what it meant to actually do it. He never let his wheelchair get in the way of what he wanted to do. He made it work with what he had. Seeing him do this showed me that I would be way better off to be thankful for what I have then to mope about what I don't, and what I had was a family who loved me.

Kayleigh: We have always said that Dad is one of the smartest people we know. He has so much knowledge on so many subjects and topics. So.... We tend to believe and trust what he tells or teaches us. Except for one time.

I was in high school and was having trouble with my car. My Dad came out to look under the hood with me and try to diagnose the problem. The car was running and he told me to grab one of the spark plugs. I asked him "Is that safe? I'm afraid it could hurt me." He said "Its fine, just grab it!" Putting my trust into action, I did what he instructed. BIG MISTAKE! I got shocked all up my right arm, it hurt briefly and tingled something awful. Of course, I responded with "you said it was fine!" He very nonchalantly said "I thought it was". While I still trust my dad's knowledge, I definitely double check things that seem a little iffy. I learned with all we know, we can sometimes still be wrong and you will only do it once.

Jordin: Growing up, it seemed like all we ever heard were life lessons and sayings to live by from our parents. Back then, they didn't seem super important, but, as I have gotten older and see the world a little differently, they hold special meanings now. Things like "teach your kids to do something for nothing or they never will" seemed really silly, but make perfect sense now as I try to teach my kids the importance of just helping someone to help them and not because of what you get in return. One of my Dad's favorite is "Prior Proper Planning Prevents Piss Poor Performances." We heard the seven P's a lot growing up. And the famous "measure twice cut once."

My parents built a new home in 2005 and moved a storage shed from their old house to the new one. It was too small to hold everything they needed it to and Dad decided he and I were going to make it bigger ourselves. We went to the store and got all the materials, he told me exactly what tools to get out, and we started. We tore the sides off to extend them out several feet on each side, put on a new roof, and rebuilt the doors. He sat outside with me everyday that we worked on it and taught me how to use a circular saw, how to cut angles, how to use a hammer, and the importance of measuring twice to cut once. He has never let the physical limitations limit what he could teach us or the fact that I am a girl limit what I could do. I am super proud of what I was able to accomplish that summer every time I look in their backyard at that storage building.

It's crazy to think how much I learned from that one project. Things like working hard and finishing what you start were obvious. But things like Love and Patience I didn't see until later. My Dad would give anything to be able to do these things himself, but, instead, he used love and patience to teach his kids how to tackle and accomplish even the biggest tasks.

Even though I don't use the power tools quite as much now, I still measure twice and cut once. Only now it's the words and actions I use with my kids like my parents used with us. I am thankful I have learned so much from my parents and hope I'm able to teach the same things to my kids.

Taylor: Humor and Hard Work are the two most important things my parents demonstrated and taught me. Humor was a choice and I was often told, "you better get a sense of humor." It would serve me well. On the other hand, working hard was not a choice. We were taught that nothing comes easy or free and that we were more than capable of doing the job ourselves.

My favorite memories with my Dad were spent one-on-one. I've always considered myself a Daddy's girl and no matter the task, I loved loading up the truck and heading to the farm. From topping tobacco, painting equipment, to bushogging, my Dad was always there supervising. Many afternoons and weekends were spent on the tractor and bushhog. I'm certain more time was spent fixing and replacing old David Brown than actual mowing. You best believe he taught me to fix every mechanical issue that didn't require a professional. My Dad didn't care that I was a girl, he only asked that I try. He was also willing to teach me anything I was willing to learn.

The ride home from the farm was always the best feeling. Although I knew I had worked hard it never failed to bring a smile to my face when my Dad would say, "You did a good job… I'm proud of you!"

Moments like those will follow me no matter what obstacles I face. I will always be willing to learn. I will always leave things better than I found them and I will always do more than what is asked of me. Thank you to my Mom and Dad for instilling these very important characteristics in me at a very young age and well into my adulthood. I love you both!

Tommy: Growing up with my parents, I constantly heard my mom tell me "You are your father's son" because, typically, I had the same response or comment to something that he would. That typically lead to us butting heads on the farm because I would think that I was right and he would think he was right when it came down to making a decision about something. Looking back now though, he was right nine-and-a-half times out of ten. I remember when Dad and I would be in an argument at the farm and all it took was him saying, "Are you ready to go to Subway?" After lunch you never would've known we disagreed about something.

My favorite part of growing up was always being side by side with Dad on the farm, whether we argued here or there or not, because that's where I learned the most. He would pick me up from school, take me home to change, and to the farm we went. However, on the weekends it was just straight to the farm. I didn't necessarily like it at the time because my friends would be doing other things while I went to work, but looking back now I wouldn't want it any other way. Quite often we wrangled my friends into coming with us because I would need an extra hand baling hay and he always had stories or lessons to teach all of us which has made me the man I am today. He always taught us that it never hurt anyone to have a strong work ethic and that one of the most important things to have was a good reputation. The best part was that my friends looked up to Dad as much as I did.

I will always be proud of how I was raised, and who I was raised by. My parents are definitely one in a million and there isn't a soul that would tell you different.

Tom and Junie with their entire family

Chapter 29

Gerry
The Matriarch

*Gerry with her family, including "The Three Wisemen,"
on her 80th Birthday.*

Editor's Note: Gerry has been involved in civil rights and disability advocacy for nearly 60 years. In 1964, as an undergraduate student at Kentucky State University, Kentucky's Historically Black University, she participated in the March on Frankfort. The March was organized by Frank Stanley, Jr., editor of the Louisville Defender newspaper, and was led by Dr. Martin Luther King, Jackie Robinson and others. The March was the catalyst for the passage of the 1966 Kentucky Civil Rights Act which Dr. King described at the time as the strongest of its kind passed by a Southern state.

I was born in Pulaski, Tennessee, the birthplace of the Ku Klux Klan. My father was a farmer who owned a lot of land. My grandfather was a powerful and well-respected man in Pulaski. I can't say that anyone ever did us any harm.

During elementary school, we moved to Louisville, interestingly, for health reasons. My mother had tuberculosis and could get better treatment in Louisville. She lived for three-and-a-half years at the now-closed Waverly Hills Sanitarium. We were one of the first families to move into Cotter Homes (a large housing project in the western part of the city, since demolished). My father got a job at the American Standard plant. We had a good life at Cotter Homes.

I was born with a bilateral hearing loss due to the RH factor of both parents. More technically, I have a Bilateral Sensori-Neural Hearing Loss, nerve deafness, now correctable by surgery with a cochlear implant. I was the oldest of four children and the only one with a disability. From the beginning, both of my parents were very supportive of my disability, especially my Mom. My father always wanted me to be as independent as possible; he understood the issues of becoming an adult. He wanted to make sure that I was able to stand on my own.

Through elementary, middle, and high school and my four undergraduate years at Kentucky State University (KSU), I had a high level of residual hearing. Only after the birth of my only child did I experience a decrease in my hearing. I started wearing a hearing aid in my left ear. In 1980, I began wearing two hearing aids because my hearing had worsened. Now I have profound hearing loss and wear two high powered digital hearing aids.

I attended the old Louisville City Schools (now merged with the Jefferson County Public Schools), a school system that was still segregated by race at the time. I must say that I received excellent services for my hearing loss in the schools in the 1950s. I always sat in the front of the classroom and was provided a lip reader. I also received accommodations at KSU. My advisor there was very supportive and again made sure I was accommodated. I also had very supportive roommates at college.

I went to Central High School in Louisville. I was a year ahead of Cassius Clay, better known today as Muhammad Ali. My sister was in his graduating class in 1960. He was a loudmouth even then, always talking, but never in a harmful way. While at KSU, I participated in the March on Frankfort in 1964. I was among a group of people who met with Dr. Martin Luther King. We had to have gotten on his nerves with all the questions we were asking him. He was very personable and down-to-earth. Later, I worked on Jesse Jackson's presidential campaign and had the opportunity to meet him. He was also very personable.

I always wanted to be a parent. I have always enjoyed being around children. At Cotter Homes, I often babysat for three different families in the building. When I graduated from KSU, I moved to Columbus, Ohio. I needed income immediately and worked two jobs, one at Lazurus Department Store and the other as a preschool teacher for a four-year-old class. Eventually, I was involved in a summer training at the University of Cincinnati for a job with the state of Ohio's Youth Employment Services and then became a social worker for Franklin County Child Welfare in Columbus. My caseload consisted of children in foster care and I made frequent trips to juvenile court. I got married and had my only child, Carla Elizabeth, at the age of 27 on September 9, 1967. My marriage ended not long after her birth, so I was essentially a single mother through her entire upbringing.

My daughter knew early on that I was different, but she never had any problems adjusting. Someone once asked her if she was ashamed of me because of my hearing loss. She was 8 or 9 at the time. She just looked at the person and asked why they would ask her such a dumb question. She finally said 'no!' My daughter once told me 'Mama, don't worry. I'll hear for you.' My hearing loss was never a problem with her. She adapted extremely well. I did more or less everything a non-disabled parent would do and sometimes more.

In her middle school years, she would be on outings with her friends and wouldn't always tell me what was going on. When I would confront her about being later than expected, she would tell me she tried to call me, but I didn't answer. That excuse didn't last long. I set a strict curfew time.

I also had a foster child for a short time when I was working at the Comprehensive Program for the Deaf in Ohio. It was a total communication program – lip reading, voice, and sign language. It served deaf individuals from all over Ohio. One deaf student stayed with Carla and I while attending the program. She was a great babysitter for my daughter.

There have been obstacles along the way to my parenting with a disability. Society's attitudes haven't helped. I remember once a woman in Ohio told me I should give my daughter up because I was divorced and hard-of-hearing. I have had other problems, too, not necessarily related to me being a parent. I went to an emergency room at a hospital in Louisville once. I told the ER nurse I was hard-of-hearing. She wrote in my file that I was 'mentally retarded.' I had to get legal counsel to have that record changed. I had a job once where a staff member passed out a printed sheet entitled 'application for a n*****'. The application had on it a person in blackface and another person eating a watermelon.

During the school busing crisis in Louisville in the mid-seventies, my daughter asked me on the way to school one day if the Klan was going to bother her. That upset me quite a bit. I was born in the birthplace of the Klan and never had a problem there, but somehow the Klan reached us in Louisville.

More recently, another hurdle has been the Coronavirus Pandemic. Masks have created a major breakdown in communication for hard-of-hearing people. I MUST read lips at ALL times. Since the Pandemic began, I have been told on one occasion that I need to start bringing someone with me for appointments. That is truly an insult. I have been independent all my life! (Editor's note: masks with transparent sections for the lips eventually became available during the Pandemic.)

My parents were always a big support for me. They taught me to feel good about myself and not to be ashamed of my hearing loss. My mother was very progressive and very proactive in getting me any services I needed. I learned from my parents how to speak up for myself. I know my rights. I have always had the support of my sisters and friends. I had extensive speech reading both in elementary and middle school. Technology has helped a great deal. Not only my hearing aids, but accessible telephones in the past, Facetime on my I-phone now, closed caption Bluetooth in my car. I remember when it came time for my daughter to move into her own bedroom, I got flashing lights so I would know when she was stirring.

There is no script for raising a child for a parent with or without a disability. My advice for a person with a disability who is thinking about parenting would be to talk to a parent who has the same disability. Talk with your family. Read books about raising a child. Be prepared for the baby. And find a good pediatrician.

Unfortunately, I still think in this day and age, most men still don't know what an enormous task being a mother is, disability or no disability. Our court system doesn't respect the role that a responsible father can play in the family. The courts continue to base their rulings on custody as if only the mother can take care of the children. Yet, in some cases, if the mother has a disability, she has to demonstrate to the Court that she is capable of caring for her child.

I look back now on a successful and satisfying life. I started working when I was fourteen, graduated from high school, completed four years at KSU with a Bachelor's Degree, received certification from the University of Cincinnati for a job with Ohio Youth Employment Services, completed a Master's Program at Webster University, and received Graduate Certification for Peer Mentoring for the Deaf and Hard of Hearing from Gallaudet University. I have had held leadership positions. I was a Coordinator for Rehabilitation Services. I was the

Associate Director and then the Director of Kentucky's Client Assistance Program (CAP) for many years. I retired from the state of Kentucky on July 31, 2015, after 20 years of service. I now serve on a variety of Boards and Commissions including the Coalition for the Homeless in Louisville, the Kentucky Commission on Deaf and Hard-of-Hearing and the Braden Board of Directors for Social Issues. In 2005, I was inducted into the Kentucky Civil Rights Hall of Fame. I have received a number of honors for my advocacy work. I have traveled widely both in the country (Washington DC many, many times) and out of it (Amsterdam, London, Paris, West Africa). I plan to go to Israel soon. I owe much of my success to my own parents and how they raised me.

My daughter and I worked together to give her a beautiful church wedding on August 21, 1993. Carla and her wonderful husband have always been so supportive of me over the years. Parenting for anyone is challenging, but unbelievably rewarding. Now I have three grandsons (my three wise men), two great-granddaughters, ages two and nine months, and one great-grandson, age five. It has been a blessing to be able to provide a loving and stable home environment for my daughter and it is a high honor to be her Mom.

Chapter 30

Ryan
Our Journey to Parenthood

Ryan, Melody and baby Ella

May 23rd, 2007. For better or worse, that date changed my life in a real and permanent way. I was riding four-wheelers with my stepdad. It was my first time ever. It was just two weeks after I graduated from college with my degree in Communication Arts and English. I had plans to go back to my alma mater, the University of the Cumberlands in Williamsburg, Kentucky, the next year to serve as a dorm director while starting graduate courses through distance learning at Gonzaga University.

We'd been riding all day along with my three-year-old half-brother and having a great time. We were starting to load up when I decided to make a loop around the sports track. I jumped a big hill, but I didn't know how to judge the throttle and I missed the landing. The ATV rolled over and bounced on top of me; my stepdad said that he saw it go flying through the air and I wasn't on it and he knew something was wrong. I flopped around on the ground for twenty minutes or so trying to get up, coughing up blood and realizing that I couldn't feel or move my legs. My stepdad called for an ambulance which took me to the local hospital. I will never forget the ER nurse who came in and said to me, "we've done everything we can do for you honey, the helicopter is on it's way." I had never been hurt so bad that even the hospital couldn't fix me!

They flew me to a nearby hospital with a trauma center where I lay in traction for four days, waiting for spinal surgery. The doctors couldn't tell my family much; they didn't know if I'd be able to use my arms or live independently, much less whether I'd ever walk again. At some point during those first few days, a doctor talked to my family and my girlfriend about working as soon as possible to try to collect and store some semen samples from me in case I wasn't able to have kids later on. In the middle of the tragedy and uncertainty, this was the farthest thing from anyone's mind.

Our First Efforts to Have a Child

Flash forward four years to September of 2011. I had just gotten married to the same girlfriend who had stuck with me since the accident. As a paraplegic who uses a wheelchair full time and has no use of my legs, we suspected that having children would be a real challenge. As soon as we were married, we started trying for a child. It was something that was really important to both of us. After months of trying with no success, I talked to a friend of mine who has quadriplegia. His wife had just given birth to their second child. He told me about his doctor, a specialist in Louisville (two and a half hours from home), who had lots of experience and great success helping people with spinal cord injuries father children. The doctor sent me for some basic sperm testing and we confirmed what I already suspected: though my body had all of the signs of having an orgasm, as produced by the automatic part of the nervous system, the part that triggered sperm to come out was paralyzed along with the rest of my lower half. This meant that there was basically no chance of conceiving naturally. He performed another test called a 'mapping' in which they took samples from all over my testicles in search of sperm production. Out of twenty-five samples, they found sperm in nine of them. The doctor thought this was a positive result; it meant that we could conceive a child, but we would have to do it through in vitro fertilization (IVF) because we'd have so few sperm to use. We met with some IVF specialists and we came to find that we were looking at nearly $50,000 for the entire procedure! With our tails tucked between our legs, we gave up on the dream of having our own child together.

After lots of discussion and hard choices, we made the decision to try some other options. We bought some donor sperm from a sperm bank from a guy who resembled me. This was a very hard thing for me from an emotional standpoint; I knew that while I would love the child just as much as if he or she were my own, the fact would always be there that the baby wouldn't quite be mine. We had the donor's medical history, for example, that we could give to our baby someday in case he or she encountered some strange genetic disease. At some point, though, this meant we'd have to explain to him or her that daddy wasn't really daddy. It took me a long time to come to terms with this, as well as with spending over $10,000 to purchase another man's sperm (we bought all we could afford at the time because we really wanted 3 children and thought it would be easiest if they could all have the same genetics). Giving up on a biological child, it seemed, was my only shot at becoming a dad.

We met with a doctor in Lexington to do intrauterine insemination (IUI). This is a procedure where they put the sperm in to a syringe, insert it into the woman's cervix, and inject it there in an attempt to fertilize the egg. To improve our chances, my wife had to take pills to stimulate her hormones. We tried and tried and tried, ultimately going through nine tries with the IUI. Statistically, most women get pregnant after four to five attempts at the most. Our doctor decided after 6 attempts that something more serious was going on. We met with a surgeon who did an exploratory surgery to look for endometriosis, which is a growth of tiny cysts that some women get on their ovaries and uterus that can keep them from becoming pregnant. The surgeon was hoping she would find some so that we would have an explanation and that she could laser it off to give us a chance at getting pregnant. Unfortunately, she found nothing wrong.

We tried just a few more IUIs before the doctor sent us to see a Reproductive Endocrinologist, or fertility doctor. This doctor was in Cincinnati, about three hours from home. They did another IUI, this time using IVF medications to try and increase our chances. Once again, the treatment failed. As hard as it was for me to come to terms with the fact that I was never going to be a biological father, we now had to grapple with what seemed like an unfair reality: my wife had fertility issues as well. Worse, these tests and trials proved that they weren't simple things to diagnose or overcome. Fifteen to 30 percent of couples who are unable to conceive are diagnosed with unexplained infertility, which simply means that they aren't able to become pregnant and that doctors really don't have an explanation. My wife's numbers were all very good, and the sperm we'd purchased was of high quality, so it was frustrating to hear that not only could we not have a child, but none of our medical team knew why and therefore there wasn't much they could do to help us overcome it.

Melody shows off a $1,050 vial of donor sperm

What About Adoption?

At this point, we really had to stop to reevaluate our plans. We'd already spent more than $20,000 on these treatments. We were thankful for the opportunity to do this because we know lots of people in our situation have to give up just because of the financial aspects. I was lucky to have a good paying job that was very supportive of the time I needed to take off in support of this journey. We were also very fortunate because my wife had been let go from her job in the middle of the IUIs and we had been able to adapt our lifestyle to allow us to make do without her having to return to work. We never had dreamed that we'd both have fertility issues and the whole experience was taking a dramatic toll on us emotionally and mentally. The false pregnancy tests month after month combined with the financial and mental aspects really had begun to put a strain on our marriage. After a lot of soul searching and debate, we decided to put our dreams of having a child on the back burner and started down the path of private adoption.

The world of private adoption felt seedy and predatory from the beginning. It's not for the faint of heart. We met with a couple of adoption agencies before settling on one. We met with a social worker a few times and developed a profile of us based on our childhoods, finances, and our home. It felt so invasive. She had to come for an "inspection" of our home. All of our adult lives, we'd heard that there were so many children out there who needed homes and that they were just waiting for good people to adopt them. What we discovered, however, was that the process was long and very expensive. After paying the agency $2,500 for our background report, we were considered ready to adopt. We'd have to pay an additional $1,500 each year to renew and update the report to stay active. Once we were on the list, we could begin the process. The way that many of these private adoption agencies work is that the parents prepare a scrapbook that shows their family and home and tells a bit of their story. The birth mothers are shown the books that most closely match with the type of home they want for their child and ultimately, these mothers get to make the decision about where their child gets placed. It doesn't matter how long a couple has been waiting on the list, for example, or how qualified they are; it all comes down to what kind of fit the birth mother determines the family to be based solely on that scrapbook. Our social worker told us that she had known of a placement where the family was chosen because they happened to have a pet with the same name as the birth mother's childhood pet. Unfortunately, this means that there is no way to know what will appeal to a birth mother or scare one away. Some families are lucky enough to be selected straight away while others wait years to even be considered seriously.

My wife sat down to make our first scrapbook and was worried about the biases people have about folks with disabilities. I had been in a wheelchair at this point for about 8 years. I worked a full-time job and did more than my fair share of the housework; cooking, cleaning, and caring for our lawn and pets. Of course, many people see folks with disabilities and assume that they just don't have the skills to be independent in the world. In our first scrapbook, my wife took great care not to include any pictures that might show me as a wheelchair user. We tried to show our home, our family, our pets... all of the things that we thought would help to 'sell' our family to a prospective birth mother. We purposefully left out anything that showed or even implied that I had a mobility impairment. It was hard work, considering how much my life in a wheelchair had become a part of who I was.

When we showed it to the social worker, however, she told us that we should seriously reconsider. She said that the birth mothers viewing the book and selecting us might feel that we were dishonest if we showed up to the hospital to pick up a newborn baby and weren't what we had represented in our book. She reminded us that the birth mother could change her mind and back out at any point in the process and that if she felt that we had lied to her, she might not allow us to have the baby. We went home and took another pass at the book, this time going the complete opposite way with it. We were careful not to include any pictures that didn't include the wheelchair or other adapted equipment. We even included a page about my ATV accident and the positivity, love and support that had gotten us through that experience. We submitted the book to the adoption agency and had it shown to dozens of moms over the space of about two years but none of them seemed to show us any interest. In the meantime, we applied for all sorts of grants and scholarships for adoptive parents. Even after the money spent to qualify, and assuming that we were selected by a birth mother, we were looking at another $35,000 or more in order to bring the baby home. This money includes fees for both our agency and the agency supporting the mother, often around $5,000 each, plus attorney's fees for drawing up the legal paperwork, and money requested by the birth mothers like health costs, help with bills, and even clothing allowances during the pregnancy.

During the two years of waiting to be selected for private adoption, we also went down the road of looking at foster care and adoption through the government's foster care system. As part of the process, we had to sign up for 30 hours of parenting classes and training. At our first class, the instructors began, 'if your goal is to adopt a newborn baby, you are in the wrong place'. They pointed out that the children that arrive in the foster care system are often a bit older or members of sibling groups that may require taking on multiple children at once. Many of these children come from backgrounds filled with abuse and neglect and required a great deal of special care considerations. In addition, there are often ongoing criminal or family court hearings concerning the children. As the foster parent, you have to take the child to all of these proceedings and listen to the prosecutors and other officials give the facts of the lives the child had before being taken away. Because the court's primary goal is family reunification, they can order at any point that the child be removed from your care and placed back with the family. Since you have to attend these court proceedings, you know exactly the kinds of conditions that these children are going back to but have no recourse to try to stop their return. We made an honest effort at the training but after 4 weeks determined that we just weren't in a position to get a child only to have them taken away and returned to an awful environment. If we had already had a child of our own, we decided, we would definitely consider opening up our home in this way, but it just wasn't a healthy way for us to continue.

To the Czech Republic

As we continued waiting and being frustrated by the private adoption process, and as our 35th birthdays drew near, we knew that we were running out of biological time to try having a child of our own. We began researching IVF once again. We asked for some advice on Facebook and a friend-of-a-friend asked us if we'd considered traveling internationally for the treatment. The person and his wife had traveled to the Czech Republic in Eastern Europe that was formerly part of communist

Czechoslovakia for their IVF treatments. On further research, we found a clinic in the small city of Zlin that was designed for IVF tourism. The facility included a clinic, a hotel, a restaurant, and a pharmacy; the staff at each of these was multilingual and were comfortable speaking English, French, Russian, and a few other languages. Although neither of us had ever traveled internationally before, even to Canada or Mexico, we decided that the cost savings outweighed our uncertainties. The clinic had a success rate comparable with any of the US clinics and despite travel costs and leave from work, we could still explore treatment for much cheaper than we'd seen here at home. We began our preparations and booked everything with our plan to fly out on October 5th, 2017, for a little under 5 weeks. This time would include stimulation drugs to encourage my wife to make as many eggs at once as possible. Then, a surgery called an egg retrieval would include the doctors using a needle to remove all of the eggs produced by each of her two ovaries. The eggs would be transferred to a petri dish and, through a process called ICSI, an individual sperm would be injected into each egg to ensure that it would be fertilized. The eggs would be incubated for 5 days to see which ones were growing well and those would be transferred back into my wife's uterus and given the chance to attach and grow just like any other naturally fertilized egg. One of the most exciting aspects is that because the costs were so much lower, we would also be able to attempt to use my sperm instead of a donor! Although we had been forced to come to terms with donor sperm up until this point in the process, we felt really great about having this option again. I would have a surgical procedure during which a piece of one of my testicles would be removed. The piece would be dissected in the lab and individual sperm would be picked out of the tissue to be used in the ICSI process.

On September 24, 2017, just over a week before we were scheduled to leave for Zlin, we were visiting some friends out of town when we got a call. Our house was on fire! I started to give our neighbor instructions on where to find the spare key in case the emergency responders needed it and she said, 'No, honey. It's too late for that'. Over the next few days, we'd learn that someone broke into my wife's car in the driveway and found her garage door opener. He used that to let himself in through the garage. He ran through our house looking for quick things to steal and made off with some loose cash and a few pills. We had video cameras around the house that uploaded video clips of him in different rooms. Once he'd found the things he wanted, he set fire to the house and left. The State Police Arson Investigator told us that he'd suspected the same man in several other fires in the area. All of our worldly possessions were destroyed, including countless irreplaceable sentimental items. He also locked our outdoor dog in the house and she perished in the fire. Without a place to go and unsure of what else to do, we decided to go ahead as scheduled with our trip overseas. At the time that we left, although the police had the identity of the suspect, he hadn't been arrested yet. We continued to be robbed daily as people helped themselves to the few possessions that we had left. Thankfully, we had great support from the community as well as our friends and family who made it easier to survive the immediate trauma.

The trip to Zlin, then, was extremely stressful. We had so much on our minds back home. Add to that being in a foreign land where we didn't speak the language well enough to go exploring, the intense hormone treatments, and the jet lag that my wife and I causing us to sleep for most of the trip, it was probably the least exciting international vacation ever. The results were very good, though; the retrieval procedure gave us 13 eggs. Nine of those were successfully fertilized through ICSI using the sperm recovered from my surgery and four developed into blastocysts, or tiny five-day-old embryos suitable for transfer. Two of them were transferred to my wife's uterus and the rest were cryogenically frozen so that we could return for them later. We flew home at the end of October.

Between the stresses of things going on at home and of being so far out of our element in Europe, the first two eggs didn't attach. We took a bit of time off to work with the county attorney as he began to prepare his case against the arsonist and to get our lives reestablished. My wife's family had inherited a piece of property with a small house on it and they allowed us to move there. Some of my family came in from out of town to help us build ramps and fix the place up to make it more accessible to me in the wheelchair. Finally, in May of 2018, we felt like we were ready to go back to Zlin after our remaining two embryos. We stayed only a few days this time. They simply defrosted the eggs and squirted them inside of the cervix using a tube. We flew home again a couple of days later.

In September, almost a year after he wrecked our lives forever, we saw our arsonist plead guilty. Once he and his lawyer saw our video evidence, they wanted to cut a deal almost immediately. He accepted 20 years in prison (five years for the fire, five years for the dog, and 10 years for being a repeat felon). Because he is a nonviolent offender, he becomes eligible for parole consideration in Kentucky after serving 25% of his sentence, or five years.

Any Options Left?

As we considered what to do next, we knew that going overseas just wasn't a viable option for us again. We knew that the stresses of international travel and being so far away from home were hurting our chances. We set out on a massive research campaign to check out every fertility clinic in the country. Finally, in November of 2018, we found one that seemed like a good fit.

CNY Fertility, located in central upstate New York, is one of the busiest and well-regarded clinics in the country. They came highly recommended and serve clients from all over the world. They are also one of the least expensive clinics we were able to find anywhere. Our treatment there cost about the same as the one we'd done in the Czech Republic.

We booked a consultation for May of 2019, the soonest they could get us in. When the time came, we loaded up in the car with our best friend from college and set off for Syracuse, New York. While we were there, we toured the high-tech facility and attached spa and met the clinic's director, Dr. Rob Kiltz. Dr. Rob is the epitome of the southern-California, new-Age doctor type. He is steadfastly committed to the Keto diet and has his own Keto plan to help ready the body to conceive. He has written books and given lectures on the topic around the world. He was extremely straightforward and optimistic, almost to a fault. We had a great visit and knew that we wanted to start right away.

By July, we had made all of our arrangements and were back in Syracuse. We moved into an extended stay hotel and settled in. CNY has a local urologist who comes in regularly who was able to collect sperm from me through a process called a punch biopsy. It is very similar to the procedure used in the Czech Republic except that they take a piece of testicular tissue using a big needle instead of doing surgery and extract the sperm from that. Since we were in the US and had our own car this time, we were a lot more comfortable getting out of the hotel to shop, eat, and see a bit of the area.

We had a great experience with the clinical staff at CNY and met with them every other day to keep an eye on our progress and make adjustments to the medication plan. It was very evident that this was a much more relaxed trip for us compared to Zlin. On July 24th, my wife had her egg retrieval procedure. I had already been in earlier that morning to provide sperm so they'd be ready to go. They told me before she went back there that the procedure was a quick one and that we'd be reunited shortly. A couple of hours later, a nurse brought her out. She was visibly shaken and distraught. The nurse informed me that the retrieval had gone according to plan and yielded just 3 eggs. When they attempted to fertilize the eggs by injecting the semen we'd collected, the eggs just disintegrated. It seemed they just weren't fully developed or mature enough. We were crushed. We stayed one more day in Syracuse to get over the shock of what had happened and then drove home.

The day after we got home, Dr. Rob called. We talked a bit about what had happened and what the causes might have been. He took lots of time with us and we never felt rushed. He answered all of our questions in as empathetic but encouraging way as possible. Finally, he announced that he wanted to bring us back to try again, free of charge, to see if we could get a different result. This was such a compassionate offer and gave us the encouragement we needed not to give up. At the end of October, 2019, we set out once again for Syracuse. We holed up in that same extended stay hotel, this time with more resolve than ever. We went through the same process, 3 weeks of daily hormone injections with ultrasounds and bloodwork every other day, until we made it back to egg retrieval.

This time, the eggs worked! They were much better quality than the last time! We retrieved nine eggs this time! The next day, we waited in agony for the call from the clinic. When they finally called us, the weight of the world was lifted off our shoulders. The nine eggs had held up to being fertilized and four of them developed into embryos. We were ecstatic and emotional. For the first time in a long, long while, we had a glimmer of hope and positivity. The celebration didn't last long because now we had another decision to make: Did we do a 'fresh' transfer and implant one of the blastocysts now, or did we allow all of them to be frozen and do that later? One side effect of the IVF medications is that the extra hormones can overstimulate the uterus and prevent the baby from attaching. On the other hand, waiting to come back meant more time away from work, more travel, and another hotel stay, not to mention that there is always some risk that the embryo won't survive the freezing and thawing process.

Ryan with his wife and Dr. Emily Cunningham, OBGYN

We decided to do a 'fresh' transfer on November 9, 2019. This means that the embryo, which had been incubating for the last five days, was transferred to my wife's uterus without ever having been frozen. After looking at the four embryos, Dr. Rob and his team chose the very strongest one and placed it. We were so excited and encouraged at this point and headed back home to await our pregnancy test results. Meanwhile, the other three embryos were cryogenically frozen so that we could try again later. We were crushed a few weeks later when a home pregnancy test showed that the embryo hadn't attached. We confirmed it with a blood test. It didn't take us long, however, to begin planning for our next transfer.

On January 6 of 2020, we returned to Syracuse once again for a Frozen Embryo Transfer, or FET. This procedure involves the team thawing one or more embryos and then inserting them into the cervix with a catheter just like before. While the science has improved greatly, even over the last few years, it can be a bit scary because there is a chance that the embryo won't survive the thawing process. Dr. Rob chose the very strongest one of our remaining embryos for transfer. It thawed perfectly and immediately began dividing and growing again.

The two-week wait after the transfer was nerve-wracking every single minute. For my wife, she was analyzing every twinge, every flutter, in her body, each one seemed like a signal that something was happening, for better or worse. At this point, we didn't even bother to do a home pregnancy test. We had already scheduled the blood test for two weeks after the transfer. The next day, a call from the lab; we were finally pregnant! I took the call because my wife was too afraid of bad news to answer it. We held each other and cried for a long, long time. This was what we'd spent years working and sacrificing for. Our first contact was my wife's gynecologist, who had provided us so much support over the years and helped us any time we needed tests or paperwork. She called us immediately and joined right along in the crying. After so many years and so many disappointments, it was hard to feel secure about things. As such, we waited several months before telling anyone outside of our immediate families about the pregnancy.

Baby Ella

What followed, though, was an absolutely perfect pregnancy. While there had been a lot of sweat, tears, money, and science poured into the process, the pregnancy was much more normal. She carried the baby well without many of the normal complications like blood pressure, sugar problems, or even the joys of throwing-up morning sickness. Because of our ages at the time of the pregnancy (she was 36 when the transfer happened and turned 37 a few months later), doctors suggested that we have genetic screening done for common genetic disorders in early April. They took a bit of DNA from the baby and analyzed it. Not only did these tests come back with no problems indicated, but the DNA analysis showed we were having a little girl! We were both so excited because we'd both hoped for a girl. We started planning and making arrangements for our daughter's arrival.

My wife went into labor on September 13, 2020. We rushed to the University of Kentucky hospital, but we didn't know what to expect because the coronavirus had impacted so much of their day-to-day operations, but we were able to stay together the entire time. She labored for nearly 16 hours with a malfunctioning epidural before it was decided that the baby would have to be delivered in an emergency cesarean surgery. I was surprised that they allowed me and my wheelchair into the operating room. Just moments after I got inside, our beautiful baby girl was born. She was 38 weeks developed, so about two weeks early. She was tiny, weighing just a bit under six pounds at the time of her birth. I was the first to hold her, delivering her to the nursery for checks and measurements while they finished up the cesarean surgery. After I got her settled, I was able to return to the operating room as they sewed up my wife's incision. After about half an hour in the post-surgery recovery area, they brought in the baby and my wife was able to hold her and bond with her for the first time.

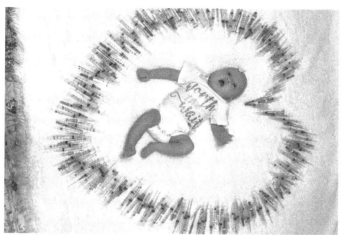

Baby Ella with the needles from the injections used in two rounds of IVF in New York

As I sit here typing this story, holding a cup of coffee in one hand and rubbing our little Ella's back with the other while playing the "Rumours" album by Fleetwood Mac for her, I am just so proud of all we overcame. The process took a toll on our mental health and definitely put a strain on our marriage at times. All told, we spent over $72,000 and 9 years trying for her. We sacrificed our time, countless hours of vacation and sick leave, our mental health (on more than one occasion), thousands of miles and hours spent in our vehicles, most of our sleep, and all of the other priorities in our lives including self-care and even our own health issues on occasion. We realize how privileged we are that we could make this journey, we've encountered so many along the way who started the infertility journey and ran in to road blocks with insurance, finances, or other insurmountable issues and had to accept the reality of not bearing children of their own. I can't imagine that there is a baby anywhere who is more wanted and more loved than our Ella. We could never have realized our dreams of parenthood without the continued help and input of an incredible team of doctors, friends, and the scores of other people who contributed to making our dream of being parents come true.